Specialties of the House

A Collection
of
Seafood Recipes

featuring

New Orleans House
Restaurants

by

Ralph and Martha Johnston
Hyde Park Publishing, Inc.

**Library of Congress Catalog Card Number:
97-077764**

**International Standard Book Number:
0-9661716-0-8**

Manufactured in the United States of America

Editors Julie Johnston and M. A. Spitz

Book Design and Layout, Christopher J. Booth

Layout enhancement, Copy Plus

Photographs, Martha S. Johnston

Authors' Photo, Keepsake Photography

Address all correspondence to:

**Hyde Park Publishing, Inc.
P. O. Box 9154
Cincinnati, Ohio 45209**

DEDICATION

Dear Readers,

This cookbook specializes in delicious fish recipes that have been collected over the years, as well as many wonderful signature recipes from the New Orleans House Restaurants. The purpose of the book is to share, enjoy and appreciate the numerous advantages of eating well. In addition to delicious fish entrees, snacks and appetizers you'll find additional recipes for mouth watering desserts and other succulent dishes that you can easily prepare in your own kitchen. It is our sincere hope that everything in the book is found by you, our readers, to be useful, helpful and enjoyable.

We dedicate this book to lovers of fish as well as to everybody who enjoys good food, good times in the kitchen and pure pleasure in the dining room. And we know, because of personal experience, that the enclosed recipes will add and enhance your cooking routine and dining pleasure, just as it has ours.

Bon appitite and enjoy,

Ralph & Martha Johnston

The Indianapolis Restaurant
8845 Township Line Road which is 1/4 mile
North of 86th Street. This is the Northwest side
of Indianapolis. (317) 872-9670.

Main Dining Room

The Louisville Restaurant
9424 Shelbyville Rd. (US 60) which is 1/4 mile East
of Hurstbourne Lane. This is on the East side of
Louisville. (502) 426-1577.

Main Dining Room

The Lexington Restaurant
1510 Newtown Pike in the Griffin Gate Shopping
Center near the Marriott Hotel. (606) 254-3474.

Main Dining Room

INTRODUCTION

In this book we are going to discuss seafood that are commonly available to us all and we will include wonderful, easy to prepare and serve, recipes for all varieties discussed. With this book you will be able to competently select, prepare and serve any and all of the common varieties as well as a few of the more unusual varieties that are sometimes only available seasonally or in particular areas of the country. We are also hoping to better inform you as to the true facts of fish as opposed to the fallacies that have become a part of American folklore.

Fish is a highly nutritious, very delicious, source of some of the most important vitamins and minerals that we all need, in fact require, on a daily basis. Unfortunately, fish as a general category, suffers greatly from poor to just plain bad public relations. That and the fact that so many people have experienced at least one bad experience, due to lack of knowledge, has for years slowed the consumption of fish considerably. A major plus on the fish side of the story, is the fact that fish includes such a really wide variety of tastes and textures that there is literally something for everyone.

In reality, fish is little different from any other fresh food purchased in your market. The operative word here being FRESH. As a matter of habit, we all squeeze, thump, sniff and look closely at almost all of the fresh vegetables that we purchase and we should do exactly the same when selecting our fish.

There are, in certain parts of the country, reputable fish markets who are acutely aware of their product and as such you never have to worry when making a purchase from them. But in much of the country we are left pretty much to our own devices and as such we owe it to ourselves and our guests to make sure we are serving only the best. It is interesting to note that the prices for a very fine fresh fish and a tainted fish are usually exactly the same. So why not get the best?

Americans eat and thoroughly enjoy a quarter million pounds of lobster each and every day. This equates to one pound of lobster for every six hundred pounds of beef served and or consumed in this country on a daily basis. This is not to say beef isn't great or that chicken is not a fine delicious thing to eat, or for that matter that pork, the other white meat, isn't a welcome addition to many dining tables. What this is saying, is that the amount of fish being consumed daily in this country is on the rise, and for seafood lovers this is a good thing. On the average, we each consume only 13 pounds of seafood yearly as opposed to 165 pounds of red meat. When one considers that a three-and-one-half-ounce serving of fish provides HALF the adult minimum daily requirement of protein while containing less than 100 calories one must wonder if, perhaps, those numbers ought not be reversed.

Fish, as opposed to just lobster, accounts for literally tons of additional seafood that is sold and consumed daily in this country. Canned tuna, a national favorite apparently, is consumed at the rate of 1.7 million pounds **daily**. Cattle growers of the country should not become alarmed, but picky eaters might want to take a slightly different view when shopping or dining out.

This has apparently already happened inasmuch as the National Marine Fisheries Service reports that the consumption of fish in this country has increased over 30 percent in the last two decades. That's the good news, the bad news is that this has happened just at the time that the annual seafood catch is declining. According to FORBES MAGAZINE, "Seafood is 'in', just as the oceans are being fished out."

But on the brighter side of the coin, we are going to be prepared for this because today fish farms are becoming more and more abundant. Fish farms are a relatively new cash crop that will save us from this impending disaster. Fish farms can and will continue to provide us with what we as a people want, need and enjoy while at the same time providing us with cleaner more palatable fish of every shape, color and description.

Fish farms today raise practically every thing that grows in water. Aquaculture is the word used to describe this new form of growing and providing us with the finest fish possible. Lest you think we're talking a pond in the back yard, you should know that enormous companies such as Coca-Cola, Ralston Purina and Campbell's have made and are continuing to make major investments in aquaculture. Would these companies let us down? Not on your life. At least, not as long as there is money to be made. You know they won't, so don't doubt for a moment that fish will continue to be available for your table as well as all of the other tables in the country.

Instead of envisioning those beautiful rainbow trout, that we all know and love, arriving fresh from a pastoral mountain stream, try picturing a commercial fish farm in Idaho, which is where the vast majority of them are raised. This is a fact that seems to have been overlooked for quite some time now. A fact that will continue, indeed increase as the years roll by. Realize, too, that fish farming has a 4,000 year history, starting in China only a short time after livestock was domesticated.

The first fish farms in America were discovered by Captain Cook when he sailed into harbor in Hawaii in 1778. At that time, Hawaiians were producing about two million pounds of fish per year, grown in special fish ponds that were designed for that purpose. So you see, this is not a new procedure nor is it unrealistic. It is a fact that fish lovers should revel in and enjoy as they delve into their next bite of that delicious, unmatched flesh of their next serving of fish.

Today, the fish farmers of our country raise over 300 million pounds of seafood for our pleasure. And this is indeed now a cash crop of major value. That 300 million pounds of fish raised in the United States translates into an industry that is now successful worldwide and doing over a billion dollars a year in business. So you see, whether you're eating rainbow trout, catfish, crayfish or oysters almost half of what you eat is farm raised. That number will increase dramatically as we move into the future. Aren't we lucky that at least one disaster in our future has been averted?

PREFACE

In 1972 a dream was realized for Deric Senecal. He had been raised in Providence, Rhode Island, and fondly remembered fresh seafood dinners from his childhood. Loving seafood, and cooking as he did, it was only natural that at the age of 50 he should follow his dream and open the first of his version of fresh seafood restaurants. This he did in Louisville, Kentucky. His dream was to have a restaurant that served an old fashioned clam bake such as he remembered so well from his younger years on the East coast.

It took a while, but with a lot of hard work, Mr. Senecal developed an unlimited seafood buffet. A buffet that is almost magical for seafood lovers. However, that was simply not enough, so he expanded and soon the buffet included a full meal for one and all. His son, Deric, smiles as he tells about his younger days working in the restaurant in Louisville.

Father and son both worked hard and while the son was bussing tables, waiting on customers and filling in wherever he was needed, the father worked in the kitchen and oversaw the entire operation. Always a cook at heart, the senior Mr. Senecal was very determined to develop new recipes and to further please his customers. Regularly or perhaps almost nightly the father asked the son to sample his latest creation. Deric, the son, remembers well that he was full to the brimming of a very rich, very delicious chocolate dessert that his father was trying to perfect.

Nightly, he would be asked to eat and tell his father what he thought of the latest offering and nightly it was never quite right.

Today, Deric, the son, still isn't sure whether he grew tired of the nightly tastings or whether his father finally hit the jackpot. At any rate, the recipe (found later in this book) has not been changed since that final testing. This is a very good thing because it is almost impossible to improve upon perfection. When the younger Deric was asked what the dessert should be called he thought for a moment and remembered that AMBROSIA was generally accepted as the food of the Gods. He well knew that this latest offering would delight them as well as it does all of us. Needless to say, the name like the recipe stuck and today you may enjoy Ambrosia in all three of the New Orleans House Restaurants. Don't miss it. And do try the following recipe for yourself.

By 1978, the chain had expanded and today you may enjoy yourself at any of three restaurants (located in Louisville and Lexington, Kentucky, and Indianapolis, Indiana,) and find the same high standards, delicious food and, yes, Ambrosia in them all. Mr. Senecal Senior passed away in 1990 but his dream lives on and is today personally watched over by his wife Louesta and youngest son, Deric. The years have seen many changes but Mr. Senecal's philosophy and dream are better than ever and that still includes his original thoughts regarding great food at a fantastic value.

All three New Orleans House Restaurants are warm, friendly places where you and your entire family may eat your fill of wonderfully prepared food, and still enjoy the casual atmosphere that suggests a different pace of life from the one you left behind when you entered the door thinking only of eating. A full bar is available and while you sit back contemplating the savory delights that await you, you'll snap right to attention when the servers come around to your table offering oysters Rockefeller, frog legs, deep fried shrimp and large mushrooms filled with escargots and warm delectable garlic butter. Not to worry if you don't get your fill of these initial offerings, the servers will return again and again, even when you are enjoying your choices from the large buffet tables.

The food at the buffet tables is self serve, so take what you like and return as many times as you want. The main table has a large selection of seafood, plus meat, vegetables and potatoes. The other tables serves salads and desserts. Remember the Ambrosia? Well, you'll find it on the third table and whatever you do save room for it as well as at least some of the other dessert presentations that are definitely too good to pass with only a nod. Take your time and try some of everything or if the mood strikes, select only one or two items and then sit back relax and enjoy and dine to your fill. Even when you select only one main entree from the buffet you will still be tempted by and will succumb to at least some of the wonderful selections that are regularly presented to you at your table.

This is a fun restaurant, a restaurant that you will want to return to time and time again, particularly when you think of seafood. Thinking of seafood reminds this writer of the crab legs and, oh yes, the frog legs and the...... well the list goes on and on but let me assure you it will always include the Ambrosia.

The recipes and the offerings have, over the years, changed and today or tomorrow you will not find all of the items listed as recipes on the buffet at any one time, but you will find tempting, delicious food prepared and served the way you like it. You will also find that times have not changed and that, even today, only the freshest and the best ingredients are used for everything that is being made available to you, the restaurant's most valuable customer. So eat and enjoy both at the restaurants and at home.

The Indianapolis restaurant is located at 8845 Township Line Rd. which is 1/4 mile North of 86th Street. This is the Northwest side of Indianapolis. (317) 872-9670.

The Louisville restaurant is located at 9424 Shelbyville Rd. (US 60) which is 1/4 mile East of Hurstbourne Lane. This is on the East side of Louisville. (502) 426-1577.

The Lexington restaurant is located at 1510 Newtown Pike in the Griffin Gate Shopping Center near to the Marriott Hotel. (606) 254-3474.

The authors would like to take this opportunity to thank the many people who made this book possible. Among them, and there are many others, Craig Christianson the kitchen manager at the Indianapolis restaurant who helped so much with the breaking down of the recipes as well as testing them for accuracy, Joan Senecal, Deric's mother, who also worked on many of the original recipes and, of course, the present Mr. & Mrs. Deric Senecal.

KNOWING YOUR FISH AND HOW TO CARE FOR IT

OR

EVERYTHING YOU NEED TO KNOW BEFORE AND AFTER MAKING YOUR SELECTION

Knowing your fresh fish BEFORE you take it home is easy and only makes good sense. Acquaint yourself with the following four rules that will tell you at once whether you are making a wise purchase or a mistake that you will undoubtedly regret when preparing your purchase at home. To do this, simply follow these simple rules using your finger, eyes and your nose.

Rule # 1

Using your finger, press the fish gently to be sure that the flesh is firm and springs back leaving no indentation. If an indentation is left, you should do the same and leave the fish behind.

Rule # 2

Look the fish squarely in the eye. Unless the fish's eyes look as clear and clean as possible, without in any way appearing dull, cloudy or retracted, it is not the fish for you.

Rule # 3

Look long and hard at the color of the fish. The gills should be bright red and the skin color should be smooth, even and typical of the species. Any unusual coloration, blemishes or spots of unexpected color speak loud and clear that this fish is not for you.

Rule # 4

Contrary to popular opinion, fresh fish smell far less like we think of fish smelling, and in fact have little or no odor. It is only when fish are old or tainted that they begin to emit "fishy" odors. Some experts suggest that instead of a "fishy" odor you should smell something approaching the smell of fresh sliced cucumber. In other words, the fish should not smell at all "fishy", and if it does this is reason enough to leave it behind.

In choosing or selecting fish to serve on your table, be very sure that you are as discriminating as is humanly possible, and then depend on the best available recipe, and Voila you are home free. Anything less than the best should never be in your home, but if through some accident it has found its way in, you should find its way out as quickly as possible. This includes any fish that leaves an odor, looks gray or shows patches of colors. If the eyes are not clear start over with a fresh fish that will leave you

shells. Hold the shell tightly and move it all the way around the shell, from hinge to hinge. Twist the knife slightly, prying open the shell and then cut the clam muscle that connects to the shell. Unless you are serving the clam on half shells, dispose of the shells. If, however, you are serving clams on the half shell use the deeper half of the shell for the server.

Allow 4 to 5 ounces of shucked clams per serving. Eighteen live clams is equal to approximately 1 pint of shucked clams. Store live clams in the refrigerator, uncovered, for no longer than 2 days. Eat or cook shucked clams as soon as possible after shucking.

For **OYSTERS** start the shucking process at the hinge side with the flat side of the shell up. When the knife is properly inserted twist the knife and then run the blade along the upper shell to seperate the muscle from the shell. Insert the knife under the oyster and sever the muscle from the bottom shell. Use the bottom shell when serving on the half shell. When opening oysters fragments of shell will likely fall into the bottom shell and should be removed before serving.

Allow 4 to 5 ounces of oysters per serving. Store live oysters in the refrigerator uncovered, for no more than 2 days. Chilled oysters open easier than room temperature oysters.

For **Scallops** you will be pleased to know that they are usually shucked immediately upon harvesting. Scallops are available fresh or frozen and smell sweet. There are essentially two sizes of scallops: the bay scallop is small and the sea scallop is

15

several times larger. They could almost be compared to the two sizes of marshmallows.

Allow 4 to 5 ounces of scallops per serving. Store fresh scallops in the refrigerator covered, for no more than 2 days.

For **MUSSELS** you must first pull out the beard. The beard consists of root-like extensions that stick out from the shell. Next scrub the shells with a stiff brush under cold running water. Shells will open when the mussels are cooked. **Discard** any that do not open.

Mussels are available in the stores frozen, live or canned. If hand selecting live mussels, only choose the ones that close tightly when lightly tapped. Mussels make a most welcome addition to many pasta dishes and their dark blue-black shell served open on the plate with the colorful muscle inside is a tempting delight for one and all.

CRAB

There are several varieties of crab available in the store and some of them are marketed under rather confusing terms. Confusing, that is, only if you don't understand the terms. Essentially, there are 5 varieties of crab. **Soft shell crab** is, in reality, a blue crab that has shed its hard shell. Caught unprepared before they have had the chance to grow another, the soft shell crab is highly desirable and makes for delicious eating as do all of the different varieties.

Blue Crabs:

Blue crabs were named for their blue claws and are the most commonly marketed variety. Their meat is tender, delicious and wonderful to eat in either the hard or soft shell stage.

Dungeness Crabs:

Dungeness Crabs are larger in size when compared to Blue Crabs and have their own distinctively rich flavor.

King Crabs:

King Crabs are the largest of the crabs and thus the name. King Crabs from Alaska average about 10 pounds in size and produce a very white meat with red edging that is about as good as anything you will ever put in your mouth. The legs are usually cooked and served in the shell just waiting to be cracked and enjoyed.

Snow Crabs:

Snow crabs are much smaller than King Crabs but also have a sweet tender meat that is most delicious.

Stone Crabs:

Stone Crabs are very rich, sweet and firm. The meat is considered a great delicacy and after enjoying one you'll know why.

Crabs are available in the store live, cooked in the

shell, cooked and frozen whole or as legs and claws and canned. Live crabs should be purchased only when they are active and smell of the fresh sea. The purchase of lump meat guarantees full firm morsels of white meat from the body of the crab. Flake meat while still delicious, is less choice and includes white meat from the rest of the body. You will also find combinations of the two and this can work very well particularly for salads or casseroles.

Allow 4 to 5 ounces of crab meat per serving. One pound of crab legs in shells is approximately equal to 6 ounces of shelled meat. Cook crabs as soon as possible, and store cooked meat in the refrigerator for not more than 2 days. You may freeze the meat, at once, for up to a month.

To clean and crack crabs, turn the crab on its back in one hand, and use the thumb of the other hand to raise the tail flap that rests on the underside of the body. The tail flap is known as the apron and should be discarded. Then begin the separation process where the apron was removed and pull the top shell away from the body and discard. Use a small knife to remove the small projections (gills) from each side of the top of the body. Then remove the internal organs and other appendages at the front of the body.

To remove the meat, twist off the legs and the claws reserving them to be cracked later. Break the body in half and remove all meat. Crack the leg and claw joints and extract the meat.

LOBSTER

Lobster is perhaps the best know and most

crisp and mushrooms are golden brown, about 10 minutes. Add dried thyme and remaining 1 teaspoon soy sauce and stir 1 minute. Remove from heat.

Pour additional vegetable oil into a large saucepan to the depth of 2" and heat to 375 degrees. Dip mussels into beaten egg white, then into bread crumbs coating completely. Working in batches, add mussels to hot vegetable oil and deep-fry until golden brown, about 30 seconds. Using a slotted spoon, transfer mussels to paper towels and drain thoroughly. Place one mussel in each shell half.

Divide mixed greens among four plates. Drizzle greens with some dressing. Sprinkle mushroom mixture over each salad, dividing evenly. Arrange mussels around salad. Serve, passing remaining salad dressing separately.

TOMATO CROWN FISH

Serves 4

Ingredients

1 1/2 lbs.	fish fillets, your choice
1 1/2 cups	water
2 Tbls.	lemon juice
2 lg.	tomatoes, (canned whole tomatoes may be substituted)
1/2	green pepper, minced
2 Tbls.	onion, minced
1/2 cup	bread crumbs
1 Tbl.	oil
1/2 tsp.	basil

Procedure

Freshen fish several minutes in mixture of water and lemon juice. Place in greased baking dish. Season with salt and pepper. Spread sliced tomatoes over fillets. Sprinkle with green pepper and onion. Mix bread crumbs, oil and basil. Sprinkle evenly over vegetables. Bake at 350 degrees for 15 minutes.

SOFTSHELL CRAB

with

TOASTED PECAN BUTTER

Serves 4

Ingredients

12	softshell blue crabs (med. size), dressed, see chapter 1
1/2 cup	flour
1/2 lb.	butter
	salt and pepper
1 cup	Pecan Butter (**recipe follows**)
1/2 cup	parsley, chopped

Procedure

Preheat oven 350 degrees.

Pat crabs dry with paper towel. Dredge in flour and shake off excess. Melt butter in large shallow pan and put in crabs, back down. Arrange crabs close but do not crowd.

Saute five minutes and turn. Saute two minutes. Remove crab and transfer to warm platter. Top each crab with 1 teaspoon pecan butter and put in preheated oven for one minute, until butter starts to melt. Remove and sprinkle all with chopped parsley.

TOASTED PECAN BUTTER

Ingredients

	pecans to toast
1/4 cup	butter
2 Tbls.	onion, chopped
1/2 tsp.	Tabasco
	lemon juice
	salt and pepper

Procedure

Arrange pecans whole or chopped on lightly buttered baking sheet. Bake at 350 degrees five minutes until golden. Remove from oven and let cool.

When cool, combine toasted pecans and all other ingredients. Place in food processor and process until smooth.

SPICED SHRIMP

Serves 6 to 8 or as canapes.

Ingredients

2 lbs.	medium shrimp, shelled and deveined
1 Tbl.	salt
4 tsps.	vegetable oil
1/2 tsp.	fresh ginger, minced
1 sm.	garlic clove, finely chopped
1 tsp.	fresh green chile pepper, minced
1 cup	scallions, minced
2 Tbls.	Oriental sesame oil
2 Tbls.	light soy sauce
2 Tbls.	rice vinegar

Procedure

Toss the shrimp with the salt thoroughly. Set aside for one hour. Rinse shrimp removing all salt and pat dry.

Heat 1 teaspoon of the vegetable oil in a wok or large skillet. Brush and swirl the oil to coat the pan. When pan is very hot add the shrimp and stir-fry, gently tossing the shrimp until they have turned pink and are beginning to char. Transfer shrimp to a bowl.

Add remaining 3 teaspoons vegetable oil to the wok or skillet, lower heat and stir-fry the ginger, garlic,

chile pepper and the scallions for a minute or two.
Pour the ingredients over the shrimp and mix well.
Add the sesame oil, soy and vinegar stirring to
combine well. Set dish aside and serve at room
temperature, or refrigerate and serve cold.

SMOKED FISH SPREAD

Ingredients

1 1/2 cups	smoked bluefish, mackerel or trout
1/2 cup	sour cream
1 Tbl.	lemon juice
1/4 cup	scallions, finely minced
	fresh ground black pepper

Procedure

Mash the fish with the sour cream until it is very finely
textured. Work in lemon juice and scallions. Season
with pepper.

Mold into your favorite shape or serve as a dip in a
small bowl with toast or crackers.

QUICK BOUILLABAISSE

Bouillabaisse always sounds like a long and complicated procedure but, in reality, it is really a very fast, very delicious, hearty stew that is appealing and delicious. You may use any combination of fish, and you'll have a treat all will enjoy. The wider the variety of fish the better the stew, so try several and don't hesitate to add a few more.

Serves 8

Ingredients

1/3 cup	olive oil
1/2 cup	onions, finely chopped
1/2 cup	leeks, finely chopped
1/2 cup	fresh fennel, finely chopped
3 cloves	garlic, minced
2 cups	tomato pulp, finely chopped and drained
2 cups	dry white wine
2 cups	fish stock
3 Tbls.	Pernod
1	bay leaf, crushed
1 tsp.	dried oregano
2 tsps.	fresh thyme, minced
1/4 tsp.	powdered saffron
	salt and fresh ground pepper to taste
4 lbs.	fresh fish, cut into bite sized chunks
	garlic croutons, **recipe follows**
2 Tbls.	fresh parsley, chopped
	sauce for garnish, **recipe follows**

Procedure

In a large heavy pot or casserole, heat the olive oil and saute the onions, leeks and fennel until soft but not brown. Add the garlic and saute until soft. Stir in the tomatoes, wine, stock and Pernod and simmer 5 minutes. Add the bay leaf, oregano and thyme. Dissolve saffron in a small amount of the hot liquid in a separate dish and then add it to the large pot. Season with salt and pepper.

With the pot simmering slowly, add the fish pieces, starting with the fattier varieties such as eel, mackerel and monkfish and continuing with the lighter fish including striped bass, sea bass, mullet and haddock. Finally, add the delicate fish, such as flounder or whiting. Allow the fish to simmer very slowly another 6 to 8 minutes. Remove from heat and serve.

To serve, place a garlic crouton in each bowl. Using a slotted spoon distribute pieces of fish over the crouton and then with a ladle add the soup. Sprinkle parsley over the top. Pass the sauce and extra croutons on the side.

Continued on next page

Garlic Croutons:

Ingredients

1 lg. loaf	French or Italian white bread, about 12 oz.
1 to 2 cloves	garlic, peeled
1/3 cup	extra-virgin olive oil

Procedure

Slice the bread into 1/2" slices. Toast the slices. Rub each slice with the garlic clove, then brush lightly with olive oil.

Sauce:

Ingredients

1/2 cup	sweet red peppers, finely chopped
1 tsp.	crushed dried hot red pepper flakes (or to taste)
1/2 cup	water
1/2 cup	soft fresh bread crumbs
4 cloves	garlic
3/4 cup	extra-virgin olive oil

Procedure

Combine the sweet and hot peppers in a small saucepan, add water and simmer until the sweet peppers are tender and the water has evaporated.

Soak the bread crumbs briefly in warm water, then squeeze out excess water. Blend the bread crumbs, peppers and garlic in a food processor. With the machine running, slowly drizzle in the olive oil and process until smooth.

LOBSTER NEWBURG

Ingredients

1 qt.	white sauce (page 171)
1/2 cup	dry Sherry
1/4 tsp.	white pepper
2 tsps.	paprika
1 tsp.	salt
1 lb.	lobster meat
2 Tbls.	butter

Procedure

Saute lobster in butter and spices. Add Sherry and let cook until all the alcohol has been cooked away. Add to the hot white sauce and mix well.

Serve over rice, pasta, or in a casserole dish with toast points.

SHRIMP and CRAB

CANNELLONI

Ingredients

Sauce:

2 Tbls.	olive oil
1 3/4 cups	onions, chopped
3 Tbls.	garlic, minced
2 lbs.	plum tomatoes, peeled, seeded and chopped
1 can	Italian-style tomatoes, 28 ozs.
1/3 cup	fresh basil, chopped and packed
2 Tbls.	fresh thyme, chopped
2 tsps.	dried oregano
2	bay leaves
1/2 tsp.	dried red pepper, crushed
3/4 cup	whipping cream
1 Tbl.	red wine vinegar

Cannelloni:

16	lasagna noodles (3 to 4" wide)
2 Tbls.	olive oil
1 1/4 cups	onion, chopped
1 Tbl.	garlic, minced
12 ozs.	uncooked shrimp, peeled, deveined and chopped
5 Tbls.	fresh basil, chopped
3/4 tsp.	dried oregano
1/4 tsp.	dried red pepper, crushed
1 1/2 cups	ricotta cheese

3/4 cup	Provolone cheese, grated
1/3 cup	Parmesan cheese, grated
6 ozs.	fresh crab meat
1	egg, beaten to blend

Procedure

Sauce: Heat oil in a large pot over medium-high heat. Add onions and garlic and saute until translucent, about 5 minutes. Mix in fresh tomatoes, canned tomatoes with their juices, basil, thyme, oregano, bay leaves and crushed red pepper and bring to a boil. Reduce heat and simmer until the sauce is reduced to a scant 5 cups, stirring occasionally, about 45 minutes. Discard bay leaves. Working in batches, puree the sauce in a blender; return to the same pot. Add cream and vinegar and simmer 15 minutes. Season to taste with salt and pepper. Refrigerate.

Cannelloni: Cook noodles in a pot of boiling salted water until almost tender. Drain. Cool in a bowl of cold water. Heat olive oil in a large skillet over medium-high heat. Add onion and garlic; saute until onion is tender, about 6 minutes. Add shrimp and saute just until opaque, about 3 minutes. Stir in basil, oregano and crushed red pepper. Cool.

continued on next page

Mix ricotta, Provolone, Parmesan, crab meat and shrimp mixture in a bowl. Season with salt and pepper. Mix in egg. Butter 13x9x2" glass baking dish. Spread generous 1 cup tomato cream sauce in bottom of dish. Drain lasagna noodles; trim to 8" lengths. Spread a scant 1/3 cup shrimp filling over each noodle, leaving 1/2" border on all sides. Starting at one short end, roll up each noodle jelly roll style. Place in a prepared pan, seam side down. Pour remaining sauce over cannelloni. Cover with foil. (Can be made one day ahead; refrigerate.)

Preheat oven to 350 degrees. Bake foil-covered cannelloni until heated through, about 45 minutes.

BAKED FISH

Ingredients

2	fish fillets, 6 oz. each, scrod or mild fish
2 parts	mayonnaise
1 part	mustard
	dry Vermouth
	lemon juice
	salt
1 med.	onion, sliced
1/4 lb.	fresh mushrooms, diced

Procedure

Saute mushrooms and onions over low heat until tender. Remove from heat and set aside.

Bake fish fillets in moderate oven until done. Cover with mushrooms and onions.

Mix mustard, mayonnaise, dry Vermouth, lemon juice and salt to taste to make sauce. Cover fillets with sauce and bake for 3 to 4 more minutes.

TILEFISH en PAPILLOT

Serves 6

Ingredients

2 lbs.	Tilefish or other meaty fillets of fish
1	juice of lemon
1 lg.	onion, finely chopped
1 clove	garlic, minced
	salt
2 1/2 cups	tomatoes, peeled and chopped
1/2 tsp.	fennel seeds, crushed
	fresh ground black pepper
1 Tbl.	vegetable oil
2/3 cup	scallions, minced
6 slices	lemon, thinly sliced

Procedure

Divide the fish into 6 equal portions and place in a dish with the lemon juice to marinate briefly. Place the onion and garlic in a heavy saucepan over very low heat, sprinkle lightly with salt, cover and cook until the onions have wilted and turned transparent, about 10 minutes. Add the tomatoes and fennel, cook briefly over high heat and season with salt and pepper.

Preheat oven to 375 degrees. Prepare six squares

of heavy duty aluminum foil large enough to enclose the fish loosely but securely. Lightly brush each piece of foil with oil. Scatter half of the scallions among each of the foil squares. Top each square with a piece of fish, then divide the tomato mixture evenly over each. Scatter the remaining scallions over the top and then top each with a thin slice of lemon.

Bake about 20 minutes. Serve by putting a package on each plate and allow your guests to open while enjoying the luscious aroma.

SWORDFISH

with

TOMATO VINAIGRETTE

Serves 8

Ingredients

2 Tbls.+1/2 cup	olive oil
1/4 cup	shallots, chopped
1 Tbl.	garlic, chopped
1 - 28 oz. can	tomatoes, diced with juices
1/4 cup	fresh basil, chopped
2 Tbls.	red wine vinegar
2 Tbls.	Balsamic vinegar
2 Tbls.	Dijon mustard
dash	Worcestershire sauce
dash	Tabasco
8	swordfish steaks, 8 ozs. each
	additional olive oil

Procedure

Heat 2 tablespoons oil in a large non-stick skillet over medium-high heat. Add shallots and garlic and saute until tender, about 3 minutes. Add tomatoes with juices and simmer until slightly thickened, about 8 minutes. Add basil, both vinegars, mustard,

Worcestershire sauce, hot pepper sauce and stir to blend. Remove from heat. Gradually whisk in remaining 1/2 cup oil. Season vinaigrette to taste with salt and pepper. (Can be prepared 4 hours. ahead. Cover and let stand at room temperature.)

Position oven rack 6" from heat source and preheat broiler. Arrange swordfish on large baking sheet. Brush with oil. Sprinkle with salt and pepper. Broil until opaque in center, about 5 minutes per side. Transfer fish to plates. Bring vinaigrette to simmer, whisking constantly. Spoon over swordfish.

SPICY CRAB and SHRIMP

SOUP

Serves 4

Ingredients

6 Tbls.	butter (3/4 stick)
1/2 cup	onion, chopped
1/2 cup	celery, chopped
4 bottles	clam juice, 8 ozs. each
1 can	diced tomatoes with juices, 14 ozs.
1 1/2 cup	tomato juice
2 Tbls.	dry Sherry
1/4 cup	pearl barley
1	bay leaf
1 Tbl.	Worcestershire sauce
1 tsp.	Old Bay Seasoning
1 tsp.	dried oregano
1/2 tsp.	garlic powder
1/2 tsp.	Tabasco
1/4 tsp.	cayenne pepper
1 lb.	uncooked med. shrimp, peeled and deveined
1/2 lb.	crab meat, picked over

Procedure

Melt butter in a heavy large saucepan over medium-high heat. Add onion and celery; saute until tender, about 6 minutes. Add clam juice, tomatoes with their juices, tomato sauce and Sherry. Bring to boil. Add next 8 ingredients. Simmer until barley is tender, stirring often, about 25 minutes. Add seafood to soup; simmer until shrimp are cooked through, about 3 minutes. Season with salt and pepper.

MOLDED SHRIMP

Ingredients

12 ozs.	shrimp, cooked, peeled and deveined
3/4 cup	celery, finely chopped
3/4 cup	onion, finely chopped
1 pkg.	cream cheese, 8 oz.
1 cup	Miracle Whip
1 cup	tomato soup, hot
1 pkg.	plain gelatin

Procedure

Mix hot undiluted soup with gelatin. Stir to dissolve gelatin. Add cream cheese and Miracle Whip. Stir well. Add remaining ingredients. Pour into a greased mold and refrigerate.

It is best to refrigerate overnight.

PEPPERCORN CRUSTED

SALMON

with

WHITE WINE SAUCE

Serves 4

Ingredients

Salmon Marinade:

1 cup	dark brown sugar, packed tightly
3 Tbls.	Kosher salt
1 Tbl.	liquid smoke
1 Tbl.	fresh ginger, grated
3	bay leaves
1 tsp.	whole allspice
4	salmon fillets
3 Tbls.	black pepper, ground
3 Tbls.	honey
	White wine sauce, **recipe follows**

Procedure

In a pot over high heat, combine first 6 ingredients plus 1 1/2 cups of water. Bring to a boil. Reduce heat to low and cook until sugar dissolves, about 5 minutes. Remove from heat and cool for 15 minutes. Place salmon fillets in glass dish, pour marinade over top. Cover tightly and refrigerate overnight. Turn the fillets at least four times while marinating.

Preheat oven to 350 degrees. Line a shallow baking pan with parchment paper. Remove salmon from marinade. Save the marinade. Pat fillets with paper towels to dry. Place fillets skin side down in pan and set aside.

Strain marinade and using only the liquid place in a pot with pepper and cook over high heat, bring to a boil. Reduce heat to low and simmer for 15 minutes. Strain, reserving pepper; discard liquid. Spread honey over tops of the fillets and sprinkle pepper over the honey.

Bake 20 to 25 minutes in preheated oven until fillets flake easily.

White Wine Sauce:

Ingredients

1 cup	dry white wine
1	shallot, minced

continued on next page

SCALLOP NICOISE

Serves one

Ingredients

3	new potatoes, cooked tender and cut into quarters
2 ozs.	red onion, thinly sliced
4	tomato wedges
1 oz.	green olives, sliced
1 oz.	nicoise olives, pitted (or black olives)
2 ozs.	green beans, cooked (or asparagus spears)
1	egg, hard boiled, quartered
2 cups	raw spinach, cleaned and stemmed
10	scallops
2 ozs.	simple mustard vinaigrette

Procedure

Heat oven to 400 degrees. Roast scallops in the oven with olive oil, salt and pepper for 10 minutes. Combine potatoes, red onion, tomato, olives, beans and scallops with the dressing, (see recipe following), and heat through in the 400 degree oven.

Arrange spinach on plate. Pour warm salad over. Garnish with egg.

__Dressing:__

Serves 12

Ingredients

2 Tbls.	Dijon mustard
1/2 cup	red wine vinegar
1 cup	olive oil
1 Tbl.	garlic, minced
1 Tbl.	capers
2 Tbls.	parsley, minced
	Salt and pepper to taste

Procedure

Combine mustard, vinegar, capers, garlic, parsley, salt and freshly ground pepper. Whisk in oil.

SMOKED SALMON

SANDWICHES

with

CAPERS and RED ONION

RELISH

Appetizer

Serves 4

Ingredients

1 cup	red onion, finely chopped
1 Tbl.	sugar
1 Tbl.	rice vinegar
4 ozs.	cream cheese, room temperature
3 Tbls.	chives, chopped
2 Tbls.	creme fraiche or sour cream
1 Tbl.	fresh dill, chopped, or 1 tsp. dried dillweed
1 Tbl.	capers, drained
12 slices	thin Danish-style pumpernickel bread (3 3/4x3 3/4x1/4" size)
6 ozs.	smoked salmon, thinly sliced

Procedure

Mix red onion, sugar and vinegar in small bowl. Let stand 10 minutes. Meanwhile, mix cream cheese, chives, creme fraiche, dill and capers in another small bowl. Spread each bread slice with about 1 tablespoon cheese mixture to cover. Divide salmon among 8 bread slices. Sprinkle about 1 tablespoon red onion mixture atop salmon on each bread slice. Top each of 4 salmon-topped bread slices with another salmon-topped bread slice, salmon side up. Top each stack with 1 cheese-covered bread slice, cheese side down, forming a total of 4 three-layer sandwiches. Cut each sandwich into 4 triangles.

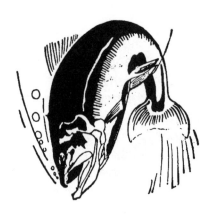

SCALLOPED OYSTERS

Ingredients

In a medium size bowl crush 100 single saltine crackers. Pour 2 ozs. melted butter over them and mix well.

oysters

Saute:

2 cups	mushrooms, chopped
1/2 cup	green onions, sliced (tops and all)
1/2 cup	green peppers, chopped
1 cup	celery, thinly sliced
	bacon bits
	cayenne pepper
	lemon juice
1 1/2 Tbls.	chicken base
3 cups	hot water
4	eggs
2 cups	whipping cream
2 cups	milk
	paprika

Procedure

Saute vegetables.

To assemble: Sprinkle a thin layer of cracker crumbs in the bottom of pan. Then lay a layer of oysters on top.

Sprinkle with sauteed vegetables and bacon bits. Then add a second layer of crumbs a little thicker than first. Then a layer of oysters and vegetables and bacon bits. Sprinkle with cayenne pepper and lemon juice. Repeat process one more time ending with another layer of crumbs.

Place chicken base in a small bowl, add very hot water. Stir with a whip, until completely dissolved and pour over top layer of crumbs. Beat eggs in a bowl and slowly add whipping cream and milk. Mix well. Pour over top. Sprinkle with paprika. Bake in 350 degree oven for about 40 minutes. Serve hot.

GRILLED SWORDFISH

with

ORANGE SALSA

Serves 6

Ingredients **Salsa**

3	oranges, peeled, white pith and seeds removed, diced
1 1/2 cups	tomatoes, seeded, chopped
1/4 cup	red onion, minced
1/4 cup	fresh parsley, chopped
2 Tbls.	fresh orange juice
2 tsps.	garlic, minced
2 tsps.	Balsamic vinegar
1 tsp.	fresh ginger, peeled and minced
1/8 tsp.	cayenne pepper
	salt and pepper to taste

Ingredients **Marinade**

3/4 cup	bottled Teriyaki sauce
2/3 cup	dry Sherry
4 tsps.	garlic, minced
2 tsps.	fresh ginger, peeled and minced
1 tsp.	oriental sesame oil

6 - 5 to 6 oz. swordfish steaks, 1" thick

Procedure

For **Salsa**: Toss all ingredients in a large bowl. Season with salt and pepper. Let stand for at least 1 hour.

For **Marinade**: Combine all 5 ingredients in a small saucepan. Bring marinade to a boil. Set aside to cool.

For **Swordfish**: Place steaks in a single layer in shallow baking dish. Pour marinade over the top of each steak. Turn over to coat evenly. Cover and refrigerate for 1 1/2 hours, turning often.

Prepare barbecue for medium-high heat. Remove fish from marinade. Grill until opaque in center, about 4 minutes per side. Remove from grill and transfer to serving platter. Drizzle a bit of salsa over each steak and serve with the balance of salsa on the side.

Combine 1 tablespoon lemon juice, 1 teaspoon mustard and the egg yolks in a bowl or blender. Beat or process until well blended. Slowly drizzle in the oil, beating or processing constantly until very thick. By hand, fold in the remaining 2 tablespoons lemon juice, 2 teaspoons mustard, the fish stock and lemon rind. Refrigerate sauce, but allow to come to room temperature before using.

ORANGEY ORANGE ROUGHY

Serves 2

Ingredients

2	orange roughy fillets, 6 to 8 ozs. each
1 cup	chicken broth
1 cup	orange juice

Procedure

Put fish fillets in a 12" skillet. Mix together chicken broth and orange juice; pour over fillets. Cover skillet. Cook over medium-high heat, basting fish occasionally with broth mixture, 5 to 8 minutes, just until fish flakes.

Do **NOT** overcook.

Garnish with twists of orange peel or chives.

BAKED SCALLOPS

with

ORANGE SECTIONS

Serves 3

Ingredients

3/4 lb.	large sea scallops
2 tsps.	olive oil
2	navel oranges, carefully peeled
3/4 lb.	small bay scallops
1 Tbl.	fresh dill, chopped

Procedure

Preheat oven to 450 degrees. Put the sea scallops
in a 9" baking dish and drizzle with olive oil. Use a
small, sharp knife to carefully cut the orange sections
from the white membrane, do this over the baking
dish so the juice is saved. Squeeze out all
remaining juice from the membrane into the dish.
Arrange the orange sections among the scallops and
bake for 8 minutes. Remove the baking dish from the
oven and turn the heat to broil. Add the remaining
bay scallops to the dish and sprinkle with dill. Broil
just until all scallops are cooked, 3 to 4 minutes.
Serve immediately.

SALMON LOAF

with

TOMATO DILL SAUCE

Serves 8

Ingredients

2 15 1/2 oz. cans	salmon, drained, picked over
1	egg, slightly beaten
1 cup	milk
1 cup	soft bread crumbs
1/2 cup	green onions, chopped
2 tsps.	dried dillweed
2 tsps.	dry mustard
	tomato dill sauce, **recipe follows**

Procedure

Flake salmon, discarding skin and bones. Combine egg and milk and then stir in the remaining ingredients except dill sauce. Mix thoroughly.

Divide salmon mixture in half. Pat salmon mixture into 2 greased loaf pans. Bake uncovered, in a 350 degree oven until done, about 35 to 40 minutes. Let stand for 5 minutes and then invert to unmold.

Tomato dill sauce:

In a saucepan, over medium heat stir together 2 - 7
3/4 oz. cans of SEMI-CONDENSED tomato soup and
1 teaspoon dried dillweed. Cook, stirring until
heated through.

To serve, slice the unmolded loaf and spoon some of
the sauce over entire loaf. Serve the balance as a
side dish to be passed.

GRILLED SCALLOPS

and PANCETTA with

BALSAMIC MIGNONETTE

Appetizer

Serves 6

Ingredients

3/4 cup	Balsamic vinegar
1/4 cup	shallots, finely chopped
2 Tbls.	dry red wine
1 tsp.	ground black pepper
18	sea scallops
18	thin slices pancetta, (Italian salt-cured bacon)
6	8 to 10 in. wooden skewers, (soak in water 30 min.)
	fresh rosemary sprigs, optional

Procedure

Prepare barbecue medium-high heat, or preheat broiler. Whisk first 4 ingredients in small bowl. Season with salt. Sprinkle scallops with salt and pepper. Cut pancetta slices into 6 to 7" lengths. Wrap 1 slice around each scallop. Thread 3 pancetta-wrapped scallops onto each skewer. Grill or broil until pancetta is brown and almost crisp and scallops are opaque in the center, about 10 minutes, turning frequently. Remove scallops from skewers. Divide Balsamic mignonette evenly among 6 shallow bowls. Place 3 scallops in each bowl. Garnish with rosemary sprigs.

<u>CHILLED CRAB</u>

<u>and</u>

<u>AVOCADO SOUP</u>

Makes one gallon

Ingredients

4 cups	Snow Crab meat
12	avocados, pitted and peeled
1	red onion
1/2	bunch fresh cilantro, (approx. 2 ozs.)
2 qts.	heavy cream
2 qts.	buttermilk
	Tabasco, salt and pepper to taste

Procedure

Puree the first four ingredients until smooth.
Combine with cream and buttermilk, season to taste.

GRILLED FRESH FISH

with

TERIYAKI GLAZE

Use your favorite fresh fish fillets.

Ingredients

4 cups	Teriyaki sauce (Kikkoman)
4 cups	pineapple juice
1/2 cup	brown sugar
1 cup	sesame seeds, toasted
1 Tbl.	ginger, ground
1/2 cup	corn starch
1 cup	cold water

Procedure

Combine first 5 ingredients in a sauce pan over medium heat stirring often. Bring to a light simmer. While this is coming to a boil, dissolve the cornstarch into the cold water in a small stainless steel bowl and whisk this into the boiling sauce. Cook 1 minute. Pour the sauce into a container and cool quickly in an ice bath. Refrigerate covered to hold for use.

Yield: 2 1/2 qts. (easily reduced)

This is a very popular sauce that adjusts well to a variety of meals. It is especially suited to fresh tuna or chicken breasts. Brush it on while grilling.

STIR-FRIED SCALLOPS

This makes an excellent first course.

Ingredients

2 Tbls.	sunflower oil
1 sm.	onion, finely chopped
1 1/2 tsps.	fresh ginger root, finely chopped
1	green chile, seeded and finely chopped
1 1/2 lbs.	fresh scallops, quartered
5 Tbls.	orange juice
2 Tbls.	lemon juice
1 Tbl.	light soy sauce
2 Tbls.	fresh coriander, chopped

Procedure

Heat wok or deep frying pan. Add oil and heat again.
Add onion and stir-fry for one minute, then add
ginger and chile. Stir-fry for 30 seconds, then add
scallops. Continue stir-frying for 3 more minutes,
then add the lemon and orange juice and soy sauce.
Stir-fry for 1 minute, then add the coriander and stir
well.

FISHSTEAKS

with

ORANGE

Serves 8

Ingredients

2 lbs.	fresh or frozen fish steaks
4 Tbls.	green onion, finely chopped
4 Tbls.	fresh orange juice
2 Tbls.	fresh lemon juice
2 Tbls.	cooking oil
2 Tbls.	catsup
1 tsp.	dried oregano, crushed
1/4 tsp.	pepper
8 slices	orange, thinly cut

Procedure

Thaw fish, if frozen. Cut into 8 serving size portions. Rinse well and dry with paper towels. For marinade, add all but the first and last ingredients to a shallow dish. Stir together well. Place steaks in dish, turning to evenly coat. Cover and place in refrigerator for 4 to 6 hours, turning occasionally.

Preheat broiler. Remove steaks from marinade, reserving the liquid. Place fish on the unheated rack of the broiler pan. Broil 4 inches from the heat source until steaks flake easily, about 4 to 6 minutes. Depending on the thickness of the steaks you may have to double the cooking time. Thicker steaks should be turned half way through the cooking time. While cooking, use the reserved marinade to baste occasionally.

Serve with slices of twisted orange on each plate.

SALMON CROQUETTES

with

CHEESE SAUCE

Serves 4

Ingredients

1	egg, beaten
1/4 cup	evaporated milk
3/4 cup	soft bread crumbs, (1 slice)
2 Tbls.	green onion, finely chopped
2 Tbls.	pimento, chopped
2 Tbls.	lemon juice
1 can	salmon, 15 oz. drained, flaked, picked over
1	egg, beaten
1 Tbl.	water
3/4 cup	saltine cracker crumbs, finely crushed
	cooking oil for deep-fat frying
	cheese sauce, **recipe follows**

Procedure

In a medium mixing bowl combine the egg and
evaporated milk. Stir in bread crumbs, green onion,
pimento and lemon juice. Add salmon and mix well.
Cover and chill thoroughly.

In a deep-fat fryer or a 2 quart saucepan, heat 2" of cooking oil to 375 degrees. Meanwhile, shape salmon mixture into 8 cone shaped croquettes. In a shallow dish, combine 1 egg and water. Dip coquettes into egg mixture. Then roll them in crushed crackers. Fry croquettes, a few at a time, for 3 to 5 minutes or until golden brown, turning once.

Remove from fat and drain on paper towels. Keep warm in a 300 degree oven while frying remaining croquettes. Prepare cheese sauce. Serve sauce over croquettes.

Cheese Sauce:

In a 1 quart saucepan melt 2 tablespoons butter. Stir in 2 tablespoons all-purpose flour and 1/8 teaspoon salt. Add 1 1/3 cups milk all at once. Cook and stir over medium heat till thickened and bubbly. Cook and stir 1 minute more. Stir in 1 cup shredded cheddar cheese and 1 tablespoon snipped chives. Cook and stir over low heat until cheese melts.

ROULADE OF SALMON

in SCALLOP MOUSSE

with

TARRAGON BUTTER SAUCE

Ingredients

1 side	salmon, (1 1/2 - 2 lbs) boned and skinned
4	sea scallops, 5 ozs. ea.
2 Tbls.	softened butter
3 ozs.	heavy cream
2 ozs.	dry white wine
	salt and pepper to taste

Scallop Mousse:

Procedure

Combine scallops, butter, wine, salt and pepper in food processor or blender. Puree lightly, then add cream. Puree until mixture is smooth and even. Do not over mix as cream will break down. Set mixture aside in refrigerator.

Prepare Salmon:

Start with fillet on cutting board. Skin side down and the belly of the fish closest to you. With a **very sharp knife** butterfly the fillet leaving the piece attached at the back of the fish. When finished cutting, you should have a piece of fish 11 to 12" long and 7 to 8" wide. It should be 3/8 to 1/2" thick. Gently turn the fish over onto a piece of waxed paper the same size as the square of fish with the skin side up.

Remove the mousse from the refrigerator and spread an even layer over the entire fish. Orient the salmon parallel to the edge of the board and gently begin to roll the fish into a pinwheel. Wrap the completed roulade in the waxed paper, set on cookie a sheet in freezer to allow roulade to set up before slicing. When fish is semi-frozen, (2 to 3 hours), remove from freezer, remove paper and slice into pieces 1" thick.

<u>Tarragon butter sauce:</u>

Ingredients

continued on next page

1 Tbl.	shallots, chopped
1 Tbl.	garlic, chopped
1 Tbl.	whole black peppercorns
2	bay leaves
	juice of one lemon
2 cups	dry white wine
1/2 cup	heavy cream
2 Tbls.	unsalted butter
2 Tbls.	fresh tarragon, chopped
	salt and pepper

Procedure

Combine first six ingredients in a heavy bottomed sauce pan. Bring to a boil and simmer until liquid is reduced by 3/4. Add cream and reduce liquid by 3/4. Whisk in butter 1 to 2 pieces at a time, making sure the butter is dissolved before adding more. When all the butter has been incorporated, strain sauce through a fine sieve, add tarragon and season to taste with salt and pepper. Hold in a warm place but not over direct heat.

At time of service, place slices of roulade in a non-reactive baking dish. Add a half cup of salted water and squeeze of lemon. Cover and place in hot oven, (425 degrees), until salmon is steamed. The mouse and salmon should be firm to touch. Lift out with spatula, arrange on plate, three slices per portion. Serve with tarragon butter sauce.

BEER BATTER FISH

Serves 4

Ingredients

1 cup	all purpose flour, plus addl. flour
1 - 12 oz.	bottle or can dark brown beer
1 tsp.	onion powder
1 1/2 lbs.	cod or other white fish fillets, cut crosswise into 1 in. wide strips
	vegetable oil for deep frying

Procedure

Place 1 cup flour in medium bowl. Gradually whisk in enough beer (1 1/4 cups) to form medium-thick smooth batter. Whisk in onion powder. (Batter can be prepared one hour ahead. Let stand at room temperature.)

Sprinkle fish with salt and pepper. Dust with additional flour. Pour enough oil into large saucepan to reach depth of 1 1/2". Heat oil to 375 degrees. Working in batches, dip fish into batter, coating completely but allowing excess batter to drip off. Add fish to oil; fry fish until cooked through and batter is deep golden brown, about 4 minutes, turning occasionally. Transfer fish to paper towels to drain. Arrange fish on platter and serve. You may want to serve with malt vinegar.

FISH STEW

with

BAY LEAVES

Serves 4

Ingredients

1 Tbl.	butter
1 med.	onion, coarsely chopped
1 stalk	celery, thinly sliced
5	bay leaves
3	garlic cloves, minced
1 1/2 cups	canned low-salt chicken broth
1 cup	fish stock or bottled clam juice
2/3 cup	dry white wine
1 lg.	carrot, peeled and sliced
2 med.	white potatoes, cut into 3/4" pieces
1 lb.	cod fillets, cut into 1" pieces
1/2 cup	whipping cream

Procedure

Melt butter in heavy saucepan over medium heat.
Add onion, celery, bay leaves and garlic. Cover and
cook until onion is very tender, stirring occasionally,
about 10 minutes. Add broth, fish stock, wine, carrots
and potatoes and bring to boil. Reduce heat and

simmer until vegetables are tender, about 15 minutes. Add fish and cream and simmer until fish is opaque in center, about 3 minutes. Season stew to taste with salt and pepper. Ladle into heated bowls and serve.

MUSSELS in WINE SAUCE

Ingredients

12	mussels, cleaned and debearded
3 cloves	garlic, minced
1/4 cup	onions, diced
1/4 cup	dry white wine
1/2 cup	parsley, chopped
1/2 tsp.	cayenne pepper

Procedure

In a deep sauce pan or casserole dish, saute garlic and onions in olive oil until brown. Add mussels, wine, parsley, and pepper. Cover, turn up heat and steam for 3 to 4 minutes.

Stir, and when mussels open, serve.

Discard any unopened mussels.

SOFTSHELL CRAB CASINO

Serves 4

Ingredients

12	softshell crabs, med. size, dressed
1/2 cup	flour
1/2 lb.	butter
	salt and pepper to taste
12	crisp toast triangles
1/2 cup	onion, finely chopped
1/2 cup	green pepper, finely chopped
1/2 cup	bacon, finely chopped

Procedure

Pat crabs dry with paper toweling. Dredge each crab in flour, shake off excess. Melt butter in a large shallow pan and add crabs with backs down. Do not crowd.* Saute over low heat for 3 to 5 minutes. Turn and saute for 2 more minutes. Remove crabs and put on warm platter. Drain butter from pan and add onion, bacon and green peppers. Saute until bacon is translucent. Arrange softshell crabs on each toast point and spoon 1 tablespoon of mixture over each crab and serve.

*If pan is too large use smaller pan and add 1/4 lb. butter and six crabs, repeat. This recipe works well with broiled clams, too.

OVEN FRIED TROUT

Serves 8

Ingredients

8	fresh pan-dressed trout fillets, 8 to 10 ozs. ea.
2/3 cup	milk
2/3 cup	fine dry bread crumbs
1/2 cup	yellow cornmeal
1 tsp.	paprika
1/2 tsp.	salt
1/4 tsp.	pepper
1/2 tsp.	garlic powder
6 Tbls.	butter, melted
2 Tbls.	lemon juice

Procedure

Rinse fish well and pat dry with paper towels. Pour milk into a shallow dish. In another dish, combine breadcrumbs, cornmeal, paprika, salt, pepper and garlic powder. First, dip fish into milk and then roll in the crumb mixture, coating on both sides. Place in a greased shallow baking pan.

Combine butter and lemon juice. Drizzle over fish. Bake pan-dressed fish in a 500 degree oven for 7 to 8 minutes or until golden in color and fish flakes easily.

SALMON

with

LEMON CHIVE CREAM SAUCE

Serves 4

Ingredients for sauce

3/4 cup	fish stock or bottled clam juice
1/3 cup	dry white wine
1/4 cup	shallots, finely chopped
1 Tbl.	dry Vermouth
1/2 cup	whipping cream
1 Tbl.	fresh lemon juice
1 Tbl.	chives, chopped

Ingredients for salmon

1	center-cut skinless salmon fillet, 1 lb.
	1/1/4 to 1/1/2" thick
	ground nutmeg
2 Tbls.	butter (1/4 stick)
	whole chives (optional)

Procedure

Combine stock, wine, shallots and Vermouth in small
saucepan. Boil until liquid is reduced to 1/2 cup,

about 10 minutes. Add cream; boil until sauce coats spoon, about 2 minutes. Add lemon juice. Strain sauce; return to saucepan. Add chopped chives. Season with salt and pepper.

Place salmon on work surface. Using a sharp knife, cut salmon on deep diagonal, (almost parallel to work surface), into eight 1/4" thick to 3/8" thick scallops. Sprinkle salmon scallops with salt and pepper. Sprinkle lightly with nutmeg.

Melt butter in a large non-stick skillet over medium-high heat. Working in batches, add salmon to skillet; cook until just opaque in center, 30 seconds per side.

Bring the sauce to boil. Divide among plates. Place salmon atop sauce. Garnish with whole chives, if desired, and serve.

CRAB CAKES

with

CHIPOTLE SAUCE

Serves 6

Ingredients

Sauce:

3/4 cup	mayonnaise
1 Tbl.	fresh lime juice
1 Tbl.	chopped roasted peppers, packed in jar
2 tsps.	minced canned chipotle chilies

Cakes:

1 cup	Masa Harina (corn tortilla mix)
12 ozs.	crab meat
1/2 cup	red bell pepper, finely chopped
6 Tbls.	mayonnaise
6 Tbls.	fresh cilantro, chopped
3 Tbls.+1 tsp.	fresh lime juice
2 tsps.	lemon peel, grated
2 Tbls.	olive oil

Procedure

For Sauce: Mix all ingredients in a bowl. Cover and refrigerate until ready to use.

For Cakes: Preheat oven to 350 degrees. Spread Masa Harina on a heavy baking sheet. Bake until lightly toasted, stirring occasionally, about 10 minutes. Cool.

Mix crab meat, pepper, mayonnaise, cilantro, lime juice and lemon peel in a medium bowl. Mix in 1/2 cup toasted Masa Harina. Season to taste with salt. Shape crab mixture into twelve 2 1/2" diameter patties, using scant 1/3 cup mixture for each. Place remaining Masa Harina in shallow dish. Add crab cakes one at a time, turning to coat. Transfer to baking sheet. (Can be prepared 4 hours ahead. Cover and refrigerate.)

Heat oil in heavy large skillet over medium-high heat. Add crab cakes in batches and cook until browned and heated through, about 2 minutes per side. Transfer to plates. Serve with sauce.

BAKED FILET OF SALMON

with

FONDUE of LEEKS and

ROASTED GARLIC

Serves 1

Ingredients

1 - 6 oz.	salmon steak cooked on one side only
4 ozs.	leeks, sliced on the diagonal
1 bulb	garlic
1	cherry tomato for garnish
	basil to taste
1 oz.	scallions
1/4 cup	butter
1 tsp.	corn starch
1 Tbl.	olive oil
1 tsp.	pink peppercorns
1/3 cup	white wine
1/2 cup	cream

Procedure

Soak the garlic cloves in warm water for a few
minutes to ease the peeling. Peel the garlic and
cook it on the stove in water to a boil, start over again

one more time. This is to tenderize the garlic and cut off too much of the flavor. Set aside.

In a non-stick skillet, warm the olive oil until it starts smoking then add the salmon, bone side down and reduce the heat. This will give a nice crisp to the fish. Add garlic to skillet. Add leeks and saute them, season with salt and pepper. Drain skillet and add white wine.

Sauce:

Bring to a boil 1/2 cup of cream, add butter in chunks. Season with salt and pepper and thicken with the corn starch diluted in a dish of water. Mix in leeks and garlic. Spoon mixture around outer edge of plate. Add salmon steak in center of plate, garnish with pink peppercorns, tomato, basil and enjoy pure pleasure.

FETTUCCINE

with

SWORD FISH

and RED WINE SAUCE

Serves 6

Ingredients

4 Tbls.	olive oil
2 lg.	onions, chopped
1 lg.	shallot, chopped
2 lg.	garlic cloves, minced
5 lg.	tomatoes, coarsely chopped
1/4 tsp.	dried crushed red pepper
1 bottle	dry red wine, 750-ml
3 sprigs	fresh parsley
2 sprigs	fresh marjoram
2 sprigs	fresh thyme
2	bay leaves
1 tsp.	sugar
1 1/2 cups	Kalamata olives, pitted, coarsely chopped
3 Tbls.	capers, drained
2 Tbls.	fresh marjoram, chopped
2 Tbls.	fresh thyme, chopped
6	sword or tuna steaks, 5 oz. ea.
12 ozs.	fettuccine

Procedure

Heat 2 tablespoons oil in a heavy large saucepan over medium-high heat. Add onions and shallots sauteing until transparent, about 5 minutes. Add garlic and saute until vegetables begin to brown, about 5 minutes longer. Add tomatoes and dried red pepper and saute 1 minute longer. Add wine, herb sprigs, bay leaves and sugar. Increase heat to high and boil until sauce is thick, stirring occasionally, about 1 hour.

Working in batches, puree sauce in blender. Strain sauce into medium saucepan. Mix in olives, capers, chopped marjoram and chopped thyme. Season with salt and pepper. SAUCE, UP TO THIS POINT, MAY BE MADE 1 DAY AHEAD. STORE IN REFRIGERATOR AND BRING TO A SIMMER BEFORE USING.

Preheat broiler. Brush fish steaks with 2 tablespoons oil. Sprinkle with salt and pepper. Broil until just opaque in center, about 4 minutes per side. Meanwhile, cook pasta per directions. Drain well and return to pot. Add sauce to pot stirring to coat all. Serve with fish steaks on top of pasta.

CURRIED SOFTSHELL CRABS

Serves 4

Ingredients

12	softshell blue crabs, dressed
6 Tbls.	butter
	flour

Curry Sauce:

4	onions, finely chopped
5 Tbls.	butter
1	apple unpeeled, coarsely chopped
2	tomatoes, chopped
2 Tbls.	curry powder
1 cup	white wine
1/2 cup	ground almonds
1 cup	heavy cream

Procedure

Make sauce first. Saute the chopped onion in butter until just creamy colored. Add apple and tomatoes, cover and simmer 1 hour. Put the puree through a coarse sieve. Add the curry power and white wine. Return to the stove and cook another 10 minutes, add the almonds and cream and bring to a boil. Remove from heat and set aside. Pat crabs dry with

paper towels. Dredge in flour and brown in butter.
Return sauce to heat and add crabs. Cook 10
minutes and serve.

SHRIMP FETTUCCINE

Ingredients

12 ozs.	fettuccine
1/2 cup	butter
1/2 cup	heavy cream
3/4 cup	Parmesan cheese, grated
1 tsp.	salt
1 tsp.	white pepper
1/2 lb.	shrimp, peeled and deveined
3 cloves	garlic, minced
1 Tbl.	parsley

Procedure

Cook fettuccine according to package instructions.
Drain well and set aside. In a large deep skillet,
saute butter, garlic, salt, and white pepper for 2
minutes. Add shrimp and cook for 2 more minutes.
Add fettuccine, heavy cream and Parmesan cheese
and toss until well blended.

Garnish with parsley.

CREAMED SMOKED SALMON

and

LEEKS

Serves 4

Ingredients

3 Tbls.	butter
4 med.	leeks, (white and pale green parts only), halved lengthwise, thinly sliced crosswise, (about 6 cups)
1/2 cup+2 Tbls.	whipping cream
6 ozs.	smoked salmon, thinly sliced, cut into 1/2" pieces
3 Tbls.	chives, chopped

Procedure

Melt butter in large non-stick skillet over medium-low heat. Add leeks; saute until tender but not brown, about 10 minutes. Add 1/2 cup cream to skillet; cook over very low heat until almost all of liquid is absorbed, stirring occasionally, about 10 minutes. Remove from heat and cool.

Preheat broiler. Butter broiler proof dish. Stir salmon into leek mixture. Transfer mixture to prepared dish. Pour 2 tablespoons cream over leek mixture. Broil until top is golden brown, watching closely to avoid burning, about 2 minutes. Sprinkle with chives.

CRAB DEMOS

Serves two, or may be served as an appetizer.

Ingredients

1 cup	real mayonnaise
4 tsps.	prepared mustard
3 tsps.	curry powder
1/2 tsp.	salt
2 tsps.	lemon juice
6 ozs.	lump crab meat
1/2 cup	wild rice, cooked
	Parmesan cheese

Procedure

Mix the mustard, curry, salt, lemon juice with the mayonnaise. Divide the wild rice into two sea shells. Cover with crab meat. Spread the above mixture over the crabmeat well. Sprinkle with grated Parmesan cheese and place in a hot oven for about 20 minutes. Serve each shell as a first course or it may be served as a luncheon dish.

CRANBERRY-GLAZED

SALMON

with

WILD RICE, HERBS

and PECANS

Serves 4

Ingredients

4 cups	water
1 cup	wild rice
1 Tbl.	olive oil
1 cup	onion, chopped
4 ozs.	fresh shiitake mushrooms, stemmed and chopped
2 tsps.	garlic, minced
1/2 cup	dried cranberries
1/4 cup	fresh parsley, chopped
1 tsp.	fresh rosemary, minced
1 tsp.	fresh thyme, minced
1 tsp.	fresh sage, minced
4	salmon fillets, 4 oz. ea.
1/4 cup	jellied cranberry sauce, canned
2 Tbls.	pecans, chopped and toasted

Procedure

Combine 4 cups water and rice in medium saucepan; bring to boil. Reduce heat and simmer uncovered until rice is tender, stirring occasionally; about 35 minutes. Drain.

Preheat oven to 400 degrees. Heat oil in a large non-stick skillet over medium heat. Add onion, shiitakes, and 1 teaspoon garlic; saute until tender, about 12 minutes Mix in rice, cranberries, parsley and half of rosemary, thyme and sage. Season with salt and pepper. Cover, remove from heat.

Meanwhile, place salmon in an 8x8x2" baking dish. Sprinkle with salt and pepper. Combine cranberry sauce, 1 teaspoon garlic and remaining herbs in a small saucepan. Stir over medium heat until smooth, about 1 minute. Spoon glaze over fish. Cover dish with foil; bake the fish until just opaque in center, about 12 minutes.

Spoon the rice onto plates. Top with the salmon. Sprinkle with pecans and serve.

ORANGE FLAVORED

CRAB CAKES

with

TOMATO RELISH

Makes about 20 cakes.

Ingredients for **Tomato Relish**

2 tsps.	Balsamic vinegar
1 tsp.	golden brown sugar
1/4 cup	shallots, chopped
1 cup	plum tomatoes, seeded and diced
1 Tbl.	fresh orange juice
1/4 tsp.	dried red pepper, crushed
1 1/2 Tbls.	fresh parsley, chopped

Ingredients for **Crab Cakes**

4 1/2 Tbls.	mayonnaise
1 lg.	egg
1 Tbl.	orange peel, grated
1 tsp.	Dijon mustard
1/2 tsp.	salt
1/4 tsp.	cayenne pepper
1 lb.	fresh crabmeat, well picked over, drained
1 cup	fresh bread crumbs
3 Tbls.	green onion, finely chopped

1 Tbl.	fresh parsley, chopped
1/3 cup	all-purpose flour
1 Tbl.	butter, or more
1 Tbl.	vegetable oil, or more

Procedure **For Tomato Relish**: Whisk vinegar and sugar in medium skillet over medium heat until sugar dissolves. Add shallots, stir just until tender, about 2 minutes. Add tomatoes, orange juice and red pepper, stir until heated through. Remove from heat. Mix in parsley. Season with salt and pepper.

Procedure **For Crab Cakes**: Blend together mayonnaise, egg, orange peel, mustard, salt and cayenne in a large bowl. Stir in crab meat, breadcrumbs, green onion and parsley. Using 2 tablespoons of mixture for each cake, form twenty 2" diameter cakes. Place on baking sheet. Cover and chill. At this point, the cakes can remain covered in the refrigerator until next day.

Place flour in a small bowl. Lightly coat each crab cake with flour. Melt 1 tablespoon butter with 1 tablespoon oil in a heavy large skillet over medium heat. Add crab cakes in batches, cook until golden brown, adding more butter and oil if needed, about 5 minutes per side. Arrange on platter and keep in 300 degree oven while cooking second batch. Spoon some relish over the top and serve with remaining relish on the side.

LOBSTER BISQUE

Serves 4

Ingredients

Including meat is optional

1	lobster, 1 1/4 lb.
1 qt.	heavy cream
1 Tbl.	butter
1/4 tsp.	salt
1/4 tsp.	white pepper
1/4 tsp.	paprika
2 Tbls.	Vermouth

Procedure

First cook the lobster.

After lobster has cooled, remove all meat and set aside. Take all shells and grind in food processor until they are 1/4" in size.

Put shells into a pot with butter and cook on medium heat for 5 to 7 minutes. Then add Vermouth and cook, stirring occasionally until Vermouth has dissipated.

Add pepper, salt and cream and cook until mixture is

steaming hot. Remove from heat and strain into another cooking pot. Put back on heat and cook for 2 to 3 minutes. Remove from heat.

Serve in bowls with a sprinkle of paprika and parsley.

Meat may be added at this point, if you choose.

CRAB MEAT CASSEROLE

Ingredients

1	green pepper, diced
1 lg.	onion, diced
1 qt.	white sauce
1/2 tsp.	salt
1/4 tsp.	pepper
1 lb.	crab meat
2 Tbls.	olive oil
	cheddar cheese

Procedure

Saute peppers, onion, spices and olive oil over medium heat until onions are transparent. **Do not burn.** Add crab meat and saute until crab meat is hot. Add white sauce and mix thoroughly until hot.

Serve in a casserole dish, topped with cheddar cheese and toast points.

LOBSTER SALAD

with

LEMONGRASS

Serves 4

Ingredients

2	live whole lobsters, 1 1/2 lbs. ea.
5 Tbls.	fresh lime or lemon juice
2 Tbls.	soy sauce
1 Tbl.	oriental sesame oil
1 Tbl.	fresh ginger, minced
2 1/2 tsps.	garlic, finely chopped
1/2 cup	vegetable oil
	salt and pepper to taste
2 cups	slender green beans
2 Tbls.	shallots, minced
2 Tbls.	lemongrass, minced
3 cups	mixed baby greens

Procedure

Cook lobsters in a pot of boiling salted water until cooked through, about 10 minutes. Transfer lobsters to a bowl of cold water to cool. Drain lobsters. Crack claws and tails. Remove meat from shells. Slice meat from tails into 1/2" thick medallions. Cover and chill up to 6 hours.

Dressing:

In a medium bowl, whisk together lime juice, soy sauce, sesame oil, ginger and garlic. Whisk in vegetable oil. Season with salt and pepper.

Cook the beans in boiling salted water only until crisp-tender, about 2 minutes. Drain. Transfer beans to bowl of ice water and cool. Drain and pat dry. Combine beans, shallots and lemongrass in a medium bowl. Add about 1/4 cup of dressing.

In another bowl, toss greens with enough dressing to coat.

To serve, divide the greens among 4 plates, divide beans and place 1/4 of them in the center of each nest of greens. Arrange lobster on the top and drizzle dressing over lobster.

MUSSELS MARINARA

Serves 4

Ingredients

2 lbs.	fresh mussels, cleaned and debearded
1 qt.	Marinara sauce - **recipe follows**
	Linguine for four

Procedure

In a 5 quart sauce pot, put mussels and Marinara sauce. Cook on medium heat until mussels are completely open. Serve over fresh hot linguine.

Marinara Sauce:

Ingredients

1 12 oz. can	tomato sauce
1 12 oz. can	whole peeled tomatoes
1 6 oz. can	tomato paste
1 lg.	onion, diced
2 Tbls.	parsley
1 Tbl.	oregano
1 Tbl.	basil
1 Tbl.	garlic, chopped
3 Tbls.	olive oil
1 Tbl.	onion powder
1/4 cup	Parmesan cheese

Procedure

Saute onions and spices in olive oil for about 3
minutes. Add tomato sauce and paste, and mix until
blended smoothly. Add the whole peeled tomato to
the mixture (crush with hands.) Add the Parmesan
cheese and cook for 35 to 40 minutes on low heat.
Stir occasionally so as not to scorch.

SMOKED SALMON SALAD

Serves 4

Ingredients

6 Tbls.	olive oil
3 Tbls.	Balsamic vinegar
6 cups	baby greens
6 ozs.	smoked salmon, thinly sliced
1 1/2 Tbls.	capers, drained
1/2 sm.	red onion, thinly sliced
16	red cherry tomatoes
16	yellow pear or cherry tomatoes

Procedure

Whisk oil and vinegar in a small bowl to blend well.
Season with salt and pepper. Place greens in a
large bowl. Toss with enough dressing to coat lightly.
Divide greens among 4 plates. Arrange smoked
salmon slices over greens on each plate, dividing
equally. Drizzle more dressing over salmon.
Sprinkle salmon with capers. Garnish salads with
red onion and red and yellow tomatoes.

NEW ENGLAND CRAB CAKES

with

HONEY DIJONAISE SAUCE

Ingredients

3 cups	crab meat
3	eggs
5 ozs.	cream
1 cup	onion, diced
1 cup	celery, minced
6 ozs.	butter
1 1/2 tsp.	salt
1 tsp.	black pepper
1 Tbl.	granulated garlic
1/2 tsp.	oregano
1/2 tsp.	basil
6 cups	bread crumbs

Procedure

Mix together crab, eggs, and cream in a bowl.

Saute butter, onion, celery and spices until onions are transparent. Mix saute items with crab mixture, then add 6 cups of bread crumbs. Work until completely mixed. (You might need to add more crumbs to get required texture.)

Next, weigh out two ounces of mixture, and form into a round 3" patty. Pat in bread crumbs and deep fry at 350 degrees for 1 1/4 minutes, or pan fry in oil over medium heat for 1 minute.

Honey Dijonaise Sauce:

Ingredients

1 cup	salad dressing
2 Tbls.	Dijon mustard
1/2 cup	honey

Procedure

Mix well together and serve over the top of crab cakes and/or on the side.

NEW ORLEANS

SPICY LEMON SHRIMP

Makes 6 main dish or 12 to 15 appetizer servings.

Ingredients

3/4 cup	unsalted butter
3/4 cup	unsalted margarine
4 cloves	garlic, minced
2 Tbls.	fresh rosemary, coarsely chopped, or 1 Tbl. dried
3 Tbls.	Worcestershire sauce
1 to 2 tsp.	Tabasco sauce
3 1/2 Tbls.	black pepper, coarsely cracked
2 tsps.	salt
3 lbs.	large shrimp, (15 to 16 per pound), in shells
2 whole	lemons, thinly sliced and seeds removed
2 Loaves	French bread, sliced

Procedure

Preheat oven to 400 degrees.

Melt butter and margarine together in a saucepan over medium heat. Remove from heat and stir in the garlic, rosemary, Worcestershire, and enough Tabasco to impart the desired spiciness. Add salt and pepper.

Place the shrimp in a large, shallow baking dish and pour the butter mixture over them. Tuck the lemon slices in and around the shrimp.

Bake the shrimp, turning them once, halfway through, and just cooked through, 20 to 25 minutes.

Place the dish of shrimp on a trivet in the center of the dining table. Let the guests serve themselves on plates and offer plenty of bread for dunking into the delicious sauce. Be sure to have an empty dish on hand for discarded shells.

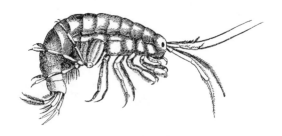

EASY NEW ENGLAND

CLAM CHOWDER

Serves 4

Ingredients

2 cans	chopped clams, 6 1/2 oz. size
2 strips	bacon, halved
2 1/2 cups	potatoes, finely chopped
1 cup	onion, chopped
1 tsp.	instant chicken base
1 tsp.	Worcestershire sauce
1/2 cup	carrots, chopped
1/2 cup	celery, chopped
1/4 tsp.	thyme, crushed
1/8 tsp.	pepper
2 cups	milk
1 cup	light cream
2 Tbls.	all-purpose flour
	Sherry wine to taste

Procedure

Drain clams reserving juice, if necessary, add water
to clam juice to equal 1 cup. Set clam juice mixture
aside. In a large sauce pan, cook bacon until crisp.
Remove bacon reserving 1 tablespoon drippings.
Drain bacon on paper towels, crumble and set aside.
In the same sauce pan combine bacon drippings,

clam juice, onion, potatoes, chicken base, Worcestershire sauce, thyme and pepper.

Heat to boiling, reduce heat, cover and simmer 10 minutes or until potatoes are tender. Slightly mash potatoes against the side of the pan with the back of a fork. Combine milk, cream and flour until smooth, add potato mixture. Cook and stir slightly until thickened and bubbly. Stir in clams and wine, return to boiling stage, reduce heat and cook 1 to 2 minutes more. Top each serving with crumbled bacon.

CORNMEAL-CRUSTED

SALMON

with

YOGURT SAUCE

Serves 2

Ingredients

2 Tbls.	cornmeal
1 Tbl.	all-purpose flour
2	salmon fillets, 6 oz. ea., skinless
2 tsps.	corn oil
	salt and pepper to taste

Procedure

Mix cornmeal and flour in shallow dish. Sprinkle
salmon with salt and pepper. Coat salmon well on
both sides with cornmeal mixture. Heat oil in a heavy
non-stick skillet over medium-high heat. Add salmon
and saute until just firm to the touch and the coating
is brown, about 4 minutes on each side. Remove
salmon to individual plates.

Sauce:

Ingredients

3 1/2 tsps.	Dijon mustard
1/2 tsp.	green peppercorns, drained and chopped
1/4 cup	yogurt
3 Tbls.	sour cream

Procedure

Place mustard and peppercorns in skillet. Whisk over medium heat for 30 seconds, mixing well. Reduce heat to low and add yogurt and sour cream. Whisk all together until just heated through. Spoon sauce around all edges of the salmon and serve.

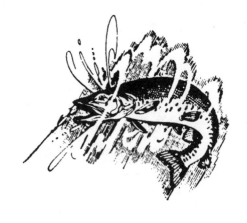

BLACKENED SALMON

with

CREAMY TOMATO SOUR

CREAM SALSA SAUCE

Serves 1

Ingredients

2 tsps.	Cajun spice
8 ozs.	salmon fillet
1 oz.	olive oil
2 ozs.	sour cream
1 oz.	mayonnaise
2 ozs.	salsa
1 oz.	green onion, chopped
1 oz.	cilantro, chopped
2 ozs.	rice, cooked

Procedure

Add Cajun spices to both sides of salmon fillet. Heat a skillet with olive oil until hot. Place salmon in the pan until brown on one side, then turn over and place in a preheated oven at 400 degrees. Cook 10 minutes or until done.

Sauce:

Mix sour cream, mayonnaise, salsa, green onion and cilantro together. Add over top of cooked salmon fillet. Serve with rice on the side.

SHRIMP NICOISE

Ingredients

8 ea.	31/35 count shrimp (tail off)
6 ozs.	white wine
2 ozs.	garlic butter
1/4 cup	mushrooms, sliced
1/4 cup	black olives, sliced
1/4 cup	tomatoes, diced
1/4 cup	onions, diced
1 Tbl.	scallions
1 tsp.	Italian seasonings
9 ozs.	angel hair pasta, cooked
	parsley, chopped as needed
1 ea.	garlic toast

Procedure

Measure the first 9 ingredients into a large saute pan. Heat on high until shrimp is cooked through. Put in cooked angel hair pasta and toss until pasta is warmed through. Serve in a pasta bowl and sprinkle with fresh parsley.

CATFISH

with

BACON AND ONIONS

Serves 4

Ingredients

4	catfish fillets, fresh or frozen pan dressed, 8 to 10 oz.
1	egg, beaten
1/4 cup	buttermilk
1/3 cup	yellow cornmeal
2 Tbls.	all-purpose flour
1/4 tsp.	salt
1/8 tsp.	pepper
6 slices	bacon
2 med.	onions, thinly sliced and separated into rings
	cooking oil for frying

Procedure

Thaw fish, if frozen. Rinse well and pat dry with paper towels. In a shallow dish, combine egg and buttermilk. In another shallow dish, combine cornmeal, flour, salt and pepper. Dip fish into egg mixture. Then roll fish in the cornmeal mixture.

In a 12" skillet cook bacon over medium-low heat for 6 to 8 minutes, until crisp, turning often. Drain on paper towels. Crumble into large pieces. Set aside.

Using the same skillet, remove all but 2 tablespoons of the drippings. Reserve the remaining drippings. Heat over medium heat. Add onions. Fry for 5 to 7 minutes or until tender but not brown, stirring often. Transfer to a 13 x 9 x 2" baking pan. Keep warm in a 300 degree oven.

In the same skillet, heat 3 tablespoons of the reserved drippings over medium heat, adding oil if needed. Add 2 of the fish. Fry for 5 to 7 minutes or until golden brown. TURN CAREFULLY. Fry other side for the same length of time. Fish should flake easily with a fork.

Drain on paper towels. Place in the pan with the onions and return pan to the oven until you place the second batch in the pan. You may need to add additional oil after the first or second batch in the frying process.

To serve, arrange fish on your serving platter and spoon onions over the top. Sprinkle crumbled bacon over the top of all.

OYSTERS ROCKEFELLER

Ingredients

25	fresh live oysters
3/4 cup	cream of celery soup
20 ozs.	frozen spinach, chopped and drained
2 1/4 cups	milk
1/4 tsp.	nutmeg
1/2 tsp.	powdered onion
3 dashes	Tabasco sauce
1 tsp.	Worcestershire sauce
1/2 tsp.	garlic, minced
1 tsp.	lemon juice
1/4 cup	bacon bits
3 cups	Swiss or cheddar cheese, grated
	Vermouth
	bread crumbs
	Parmesan cheese

Procedure

Squeeze water from spinach before adding to the sauce. Mix all ingredients except oysters together well. Heat on medium heat until cheese melts. Stir to prevent sticking and scorching, or use a double boiler. Allow sauce to cool in refrigerator. Shuck oysters. Place them on an oven proof tray. Spoon sauce over oysters. Sprinkle with bread crumbs and Parmesan cheese. Bake in oven at 400 degrees for 10 to 15 minutes or until lightly brown. Remove from oven and mist the oysters with dry Vermouth.

NEW ENGLAND

FISH CHOWDER

Ingredients

4 ozs.	salt pork, diced small
5 lg.	potatoes, peeled and diced
1 lg.	onion, diced
1 qt.	milk
1/2 tsp.	black pepper
2 tsps.	butter
1 lb.	white fish, cod, pollock or haddock

Procedure

Saute salt pork on medium heat until reduced to crunchy little pieces. **Do not burn.** Remove pork from grease and set aside.

In a separate 5 quart pot, put potatoes, onion and pepper.

Then add enough hot water to cover an inch over vegetables. Cook on high heat. When potato is half cooked, add fish and salt pork and cook until fish and potatoes are done.

Add 1 quart milk and butter. Cook until hot and serve.

MOUSSE OF SCALLOPS

with

SAFFRON

Ingredients

1/4 lb.	fresh scallops
1/3 cup	heavy cream
4	egg whites
1 pinch	saffron
	salt and pepper to taste
1/4 cup	butter
1 sm.	zucchini

Procedure

In a food processor, grind the scallops. Keep in a bowl on ice and with a rubber spatula add the cream and egg whites one by one. Season with salt and pepper to taste and add saffron.

With a "channel knife" stripe the zucchini and slice it very finely. Place zucchini slices around the edge of a very well greased souffle cup, then add the scallop batter to it.

Bake at 350 degrees for 20 minutes in a double boiler, water bath.

137

FRESH FISH

with

SESAME TERIYAKI LINGUINE

Ingredients

9 ozs.	linguine, cooked
2 ozs.	sesame oil
4 ozs.	sesame teriyaki glaze (see index for recipe)
1/4 cup	snow peas
1/4 cup	almonds, sliced
6 ozs.	fresh fish filet (tuna is best)

Procedure

Heat the sesame oil and the sesame teriyaki glaze together in a large saute pan. When sauce is hot, toss in linguine, snow peas, and almonds. Heat through, but let the snow peas remain crisp. Top with a nice piece of grilled tuna that has been brushed with the sesame teriyaki glaze. You can substitute any fish filet or even a chicken breast for this dish.

FISH and CHEESE

Serves 4

Ingredients

1 lb.	fresh or frozen fish fillets
1	egg, beaten
2 Tbls.	milk
1/4 cup	Parmesan cheese, grated
1/4 cup	wheat wafers, finely crushed
1/2 tsp.	dried basil, crushed
1/2 tsp.	paprika
1/8 tsp.	pepper
2 Tbls.	cooking oil

Procedure

Thaw fish, if frozen. Separate fillets into serving size portions. Rinse well and pat dry with a paper towel. In a shallow dish, combine the egg and milk. In another shallow dish, combine the cheese, crushed wafers, basil, paprika and pepper.

Dip fish into egg mixture. Then roll in crumb mixture. Place coated fish in a greased shallow baking pan. Drizzle oil over fish. Bake in a 500 degree oven until golden brown and fish flakes easily, about 5 to 6 minutes for each half inch of thickness of fillets.

SALMON TOMATO SAUTE'

with

LINGUINE

Serves 4

Ingredients

1 lb.	salmon, cut into 3/4" chunks
1 bunch	watercress, cleaned and chopped into1" pieces
20	sun-dried tomato slices, soaked in warm water for 1 hour
5 lg.	cloves garlic, minced
1/2 cup	shallots
1/8 cup	white wine
	enough cooked linguine for 4 people
	salt and pepper to taste
	olive oil

Procedure

Mix shallots, garlic and wine together in a bowl and soak for 10 minutes. With a large saute pan on medium high heat, add 3 tablespoons of olive oil. Once hot, add salmon and saute until 3/4 done. Add tomatoes and heat for 15 seconds. Add the shallot mixture and heat for another 15 seconds. Add watercress and heat until al dente'. Remove from heat and serve over cooked linguine.

SCALLOP ALFREDO

Ingredients

1/2 qt.	heavy cream
1 cup	sour cream
1/2 tsp.	salt
1 cup	Parmesan cheese
1 tsp.	butter
1 tsp.	granulated garlic
1 tsp.	onion powder
1 cup	scallops, chopped
1 tsp.	lemon juice
1 1/2 Tbls.	Vermouth

Procedure

Cook enough pasta (your favorite) for 4 people.

In a large saute pan, add heavy cream, salt, garlic, onion powder and heat until steamy hot. Next, add sour cream and mix until all are dissolved. Add Parmesan cheese, mix well, and set aside.

In another saute pan, add butter and scallops. Cook until scallops are reduced and liquid comes out. Remove from heat, drain liquid and put back on heat.

Add Vermouth. Heat for 2 minutes. Remove from heat and add to sauce. Serve sauce over cooked pasta.

SPICY PRAWNS

Serves 4

Ingredients

1 lb.	prawns, peeled
6 Tbls.	lemon juice
6	spring onions, sliced
2 tsps.	fresh ginger root, finely chopped
1 stem	lemon grass, finely chopped
2 Tbls.	fresh mint, chopped
4 med.	lettuce leaves
	sprigs of lemon grass

Serve the prawns in scallop shells.

Procedure

Put the prawns into a bowl and pour the lemon juice over. Stir in the spring onions, ginger, lemon grass and mint. Stir well to mix thoroughly. Cover and chill in refrigerator for 3 hours, stirring once or twice.

To serve, place a lettuce leaf in each of the four scallop shells and pile the prawn mixture on top.

Add a sprig of lemon grass for garnish.

BROILED FILLETS

with

FRESH MINT

Serves 4

Ingredients

1 lb.	fresh or frozen fish fillets
3 Tbls.	butter, melted
1 Tbl.	onion, finely chopped
1 Tbl.	fresh mint, finely chopped
1 Tbl.	lime juice
1 clove	garlic, minced
1/4 tsp.	salt
dash	pepper

Procedure

Thaw fillets, if frozen. Cut into 4 portions. Rinse fillets well and dry with paper towels.

Basting Sauce:

In a small mixing bowl, combine butter, onion, chopped mint, lime juice, garlic, salt and pepper. Set aside.

Preheat broiler. Place fillets on the unheated rack of a broiler pan. Fold any thin edges under. Brush fillets with the basting sauce. Broil 4 inches from heat until fillets flake easily when probed. Allow 4 to 6 minutes for each 1/2" of thickness. If fillets are thicker than 1 inch, turn when half done. Brush fillets occasionally with additional basting sauce.

Use lemon wedges and fresh mint sprigs for garnish.

BROILED SALMON

with

ROSEMARY

Serves 4

Ingredients

1 lb.	fresh or frozen salmon fillets or steaks
1/4 cup	dry white wine
2 Tbls.	cooking oil
1/2 tsp.	lemon peel, finely shredded
1 Tbl.	lemon juice
1 Tbl.	Worcestershire sauce
1/2 tsp.	dried rosemary, crushed
1 sm. clove	garlic, minced

Procedure

Thaw fish, if frozen. Separate into 4 serving size
portions. Rinse and pat dry with paper towels. For
marinade: in a shallow dish combine dry white
wine, oil, lemon peel, lemon juice, Worcestershire,
rosemary, and garlic. Add fish; cover and let stand at
room temperature for 1 hour, turning occasionally.

Preheat broiler. Drain fish, reserving marinade.

Measure thickness of fish. Place fish on the unheated rack of a broiler pan. If using fillets, tuck under any thin edges. Broil 4" from heat till fish flakes easily with a fork.

Allow 4 to 6 minutes for each 1/2" of thickness. Brush occasionally with reserved marinade. If fish is 1" or thicker, turn when half done.

SHRIMP on a STICK

Makes 24 appetizers

Ingredients

24	fresh or frozen shelled shrimp, med. size
1/4 cup	onion, finely chopped
1 Tbl.	cooking oil
1/3 cup	chili sauce
2 Tbls.	water
2 tsps.	vinegar
2 tsps.	Worcestershire sauce
1/2 tsp.	dry mustard
dash	ground red pepper

Procedure

Thaw shrimp, if frozen. Rinse and pat dry with paper towels. Set aside. For basting sauce: in a saucepan cook onion in hot oil over medium-high heat until tender, stirring often. Stir in chili sauce, water, vinegar, Worcestershire, dry mustard, and red pepper; simmer uncovered, about 8 minutes or until slightly thickened, stirring occasionally.

Meanwhile, preheat broiler. Thread shrimp on short skewers. Place on the unheated rack of a broiler pan. Broil 4 inches from heat about 4 minutes or until shrimp turn pink, turning skewers and brushing shrimp occasionally with basting sauce.

SEAFOOD DIABLO

Serves 4 to 6

Ingredients

4 ea.	31/35 count shrimp (tail off)
4 ea.	scallops
2 1/2 ozs.	calamari rings, (Squid)
2 ozs.	clam juice
2 ozs.	white wine
2 ozs.	garlic butter
1/4 cup	mushrooms, sliced
2 Tbls.	scallions
1 tsp.	crushed red pepper
3 ozs.	marinara sauce
9 ozs.	angel hair pasta, cooked
	shredded Parmesan cheese (fresh), as needed
	chopped parsley, as needed
1 ea.	garlic toast

Procedure

Each items = per persons served.

Measure the first 10 ingredients into a large saute pan. Heat on high until the seafood is cooked through. Toss often. Do not allow to dry out. When seafood is cooked, put in precooked pasta and toss until pasta is warmed thoroughly. Serve in a pasta bowl, and top with Parmesan cheese and a sprinkling of parsley and a slice of garlic toast.

SEAFOOD FETTUCCINE

Serves one

Ingredients

1 oz.	olive oil
1 Tbl.	garlic, shaved
3	shrimp, split, tails removed
2 ozs.	clams, chopped
2 ozs.	carrots, chopped
2 ozs.	tomatoes, diced
2 ozs.	white wine
1 Tbl.	basil, julienned
1/2 cup	heavy cream
2 ozs.	Parmesan cheese, shredded
4 ozs.	butter
1 oz.	arugala
10 ozs.	fettuccine
3	clams, littleneck
1 tsp.	parsley, chopped

Procedure

Preheat pan with oil for thirty seconds. Add garlic and cook until lightly brown. Next, add shrimp, clams, carrots and tomatoes. Cook for 45 seconds, toss to coat. Add white wine and reduce by half, then add basil. After wine is reduced, add heavy cream and reduce by 1/4, then add Parmesan, butter and arugala.

Place drained pasta and littleneck clams in pan and toss to coat. Place pasta on serving plate, pour remaining sauce and ingredients over top. Place littleneck clams around the pasta. Garnish with parsley.

SHRIMP SCAMPI

Serves 1

Ingredients

16 - 20	shrimp
1/4 cup	flour
1 oz.	salt
1 oz.	pepper
2 ozs.	olive oil
1 oz.	butter, unsalted
1 oz.	white wine
1/4 tsp.	garlic, chopped
	lemon to taste
1/2 cup	linguine, cooked

Procedure

Peel and clean shrimp, then pat dry. Coat shrimp with flour mixed with salt and pepper. Heat a skillet with olive oil until hot, add shrimp one piece at a time. Let brown on one side and then place in preheated oven 375 degrees for three minutes.

For sauce: In a small skillet mix unsalted butter, white wine, garlic and lemon until all are melted and creamy. Place shrimp over hot linguine and pour sauce over top of the shrimp.

HERB-COATED CRAB CAKES

Makes 8

Ingredients

3 cups	whole wheat bread, crusts trimmed, diced
1/4 cup	fresh chives, coarsely chopped
1/4 cup	fresh parsley, coarsely chopped
1/4 tsp.	ground black pepper
3 Tbls.	butter, or more
1/4 cup	green onions, finely chopped
1/4 cup	red bell pepper, finely chopped
1 tsp.	garlic, minced
1 Tbl.	all purpose flour
6 Tbls.	whipping cream
3 Tbls.	fresh basil, minced or 1 Tbl. dried
1 lg.	egg yolk, beaten to blend
1 Tbl.	Dijon mustard
2 tsps.	fresh lemon juice
1 1/2 tsps.	hot chili sauce, (such as Sriracha)
3/4 tsp.	salt
12 ozs.	crab meat, well drained, picked over

Procedure

Finely grind first 4 ingredients in processor. Set aside.

Melt 1 tablespoon butter in a heavy large skillet over medium heat. Add green onions, bell pepper and garlic; saute 1 minute. Add flour; stir 1 minute longer. Gradually, whisk in cream. Increase heat to medium-high and whisk until mixture thickens slightly, about 1 minute. Remove from heat. Mix in basil, egg yolk, mustard, lemon juice, chili sauce and salt. Transfer to a large bowl. Stir in crab meat and 1/4 cup breadcrumb mixture.

Form crab mixture into 1/2" thick cakes, using approximately 1/4 cup for each. Place remaining breadcrumb mixture into a shallow bowl. Coat each crab cake with breadcrumb mixture, pressing gently to adhere. (Can be prepared 1 hour ahead. Arrange cakes on baking sheet. Cover with plastic and refrigerate.)

Melt 2 tablespoons butter in a large non-stick skillet over medium-high heat. Working in batches, add the crab cakes to skillet and cook until golden brown, adding more butter to skillet as necessary, about 3 minutes per side. Transfer cakes to a platter and serve.

BAKED SALMON

with

MUSTARD and TARRAGON

Serves 4

Ingredients

1 - 1 1/2 lb.	center-cut salmon fillet, with skin
1/2 cup	mayonnaise
2 Tbls.	Dijon mustard
2 Tbls.	fresh tarragon, chopped, or 2 tsp. dried
1/4 tsp.	white wine vinegar
	lemon wedges

Procedure

Preheat oven to 350 degrees. Place salmon, skin side down, in ungreased roasting pan. Sprinkle with salt and pepper. Whisk mayonnaise, mustard, tarragon and vinegar in a small bowl to blend, season topping to taste with salt and pepper. Spread topping over top and sides of salmon, covering completely. Cover pan tightly with heavy-duty aluminum foil.

Bake salmon covered until almost cooked through,

(salmon will still feel almost firm when pressed with finger), about 35 minutes Remove from oven; preheat broiler. Uncover pan and broil until topping is deep golden brown and salmon feels firm to touch, about 5 minutes. Cut salmon crosswise into 4 pieces. Slide spatula between salmon and skin and transfer salmon pieces to plates. Serve with lemon wedges.

TUNA WALDORF SALAD

Serves 4

Ingredients

2 cans	tuna, 9 1/4 oz. ea.
2 large	apples, cored and chopped
2/3 cup	celery, chopped
2/3 cup	walnuts, chopped
2/3 cup	raisins
1 cup	dairy sour cream
1/2 cup	mayonnaise
2 Tbls.	lemon juice
	leaf lettuce
4 ozs.	cheddar cheese, shredded

Procedure

Drain tuna and break into chunks. Combine tuna, apples, celery, walnuts and raisins and set aside.

In another bowl, combine sour cream, mayonnaise and lemon juice. Mix well. Add bowl of dressing mix to bowl of tuna and mix well. Chill.

To serve, place lettuce leaves on plate, sprinkle with cheese before adding tuna salad.

ADDITIONAL

NEW ORLEANS HOUSE

RESTAURANTS

RECIPES

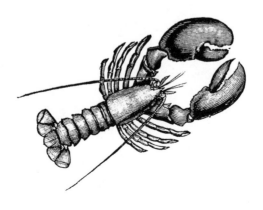

CHICKEN ROUXARD

with

ROASTED GARLIC BUTTER

SAUCE

Prep time - 90 Minutes

Serves 6

Ingredients

6	chicken breasts, 8 ozs. ea., boneless and skinless

Stuffing:

1 lb.	Italian sausage, chopped fine
2 stalks	celery
1 med.	onion
1 tsp.	garlic, chopped
1/2 med.	green pepper
1/4 med.	red pepper
2 tsp.	Tabasco
1/8 cup	Worcestershire sauce
2 tsp.	New Orleans House Cajun Spice
1/4 cup	chicken stock
	bread crumbs

Procedure

Saute finely chopped sausage in a pan until cooked thoroughly, but not browned. Remove from grease and set aside.

Place celery, onion, peppers and garlic in a food processor and puree until smooth.

Mix together in a large mixing bowl, sausage mixture, vegetable mixture, Tabasco, Worcestershire, New Orleans House Spice and chicken stock until mixed thoroughly. Then, add enough bread crumbs until you get a stuffing like texture.

Chicken:

Trim all fat from chicken breast. Pound the chicken breast flat and thin. Once the chicken is pounded, lay one breast out flat (smooth side down). Put 5 tablespoons of stuffing mixture on breast and smooth out evenly across the whole breast.

Next, roll the breast into a roll. Trim the edges and bake at 350 degrees for 25 minutes. Sticking a toothpick in the rolled breast will keep it held together.

continued on next page

Sauce for Chicken Rouxard:

5 lg. cloves	garlic
1/2 bunch	shallots, coarse chopped
5	bay leaves
1 tsp.	thyme
1/4 tsp.	pepper
2 cups	light chicken stock
5 tsp.	cold butter

Crush garlic and chop fine. Put in small saute pan and cook with no butter until garlic is brown. Remove and place garlic in a 2 quart sauce pan. Add shallots and spices and cook for 1 minute. Add chicken stock and reduce by half. Add butter and stir until you get the consistency of gravy. Remove from heat and top the chicken.

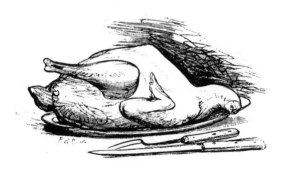

NEW ORLEANS CHICKEN

Ingredients

8 to 10	chicken thighs
2 bunches	green onions, minced
10 cloves	fresh garlic, minced
	ginger root, amount equal to garlic
1/2 cup	sugar
1/2 tsp.	white pepper
1/2 tsp.	sesame oil
1 1/2 cups	soy sauce

Procedure

Remove the skin from chicken thighs. Score the thighs three times with a knife on the meaty side. Turn the thighs over and pull out the meat on each side of the bone.

Mix the minced vegetables and other ingredients together in a casserole dish. Add the chicken thighs and let them marinate in the refrigerator for four hours or longer. When ready to cook, place chicken thighs on a sheet pan and bake for twenty minutes.

Remove from oven.

Turn chicken over and broil for 5 to 10 minutes.

CAJUN GUMBO & ANDOUILLE

SAUSAGE

About Andouille Sausage: It is a Cajun spiced Smoked Sausage, mostly beef. It does have some pork. Gourmet shops may carry it. Sometimes it is hard to find. You may substitute with a Kielbasa.

Ingredients

Seasoning Mix:

1 Tbl.	thyme
1 Tbl.	white pepper
1 tsp.	cayenne pepper
1 tsp.	oregano
1/2 Tbl.	granulated garlic

Additional Ingredients

1 lb.	red beans
1 cup	ham & ham bone
1/4 cup	molasses
2 cups	onion, chopped
2 cups	green pepper, chopped
2 1/2 cups	celery, chopped
3/4 lbs.	sausage, sliced
1 Tbl.	Tabasco
1/2 cup	green onion, finely chopped
1/2 cup	seasoned rice
2	bay leaves
	green onion, finely chopped

The night before, cover beans with 2" of water in a bowl and let stand.

Place 2 1/2 quarts water in sauce pan. Add ham bone, celery, onions, peppers, bay leaves, seasoning mix and beans. Bring to a boil. Reduce heat and simmer for 1 hour. Transfer to a large deep baking dish. Stir in molasses, Tabasco, ham meat from bone and sausage. Discard bone. Bake at 350 degrees for 1 hour. Stir occasionally, remove from heat and stir in 1/2 cup of seasoned cooked rice. Sprinkle with finely chopped green onions.

BAYOU GREEN BEANS

Ingredients

2 lbs.	whole green beans
1	ham hock or trimmings
4 cups	boiling water
1/4 tsp.	black pepper
1 tsp.	sugar
2 lg.	red peppers, diced

Procedure

Wash and tip green beans and break in half. Place water in a sauce pan. Boil and add sugar, pepper, beans and ham. Bring to a boil, then lower heat and cook for one hour. Add diced red peppers and cook another 30 minutes.

You may cook beans for a longer or shorter time, depending on how you like your beans.

STUFFED CELERY

Ingredients

1 lb.	cream cheese
1 Tbl.	lemon juice
1 tsp.	Worcestershire sauce
1/2 cup	pimentos, chopped
10 to 12 ribs	celery

Procedure

Mix first four ingredients together well. Cut celery into thirds, about 4 inches long. Place mixture in a pastry bag and squeeze into the canal of the celery.

This makes about thirty pieces. A great party appetizer.

Tip:

You may choose to fill a plastic storage bag with mixture and simply cut off a corner to desired size and use this instead of a pastry bag. This also works well to create designs or writing.

FRENCH ONION SOUP

Serves 4 to 6

Ingredients

4 lg.	Spanish onions, cut to julienne
5 Tbls.	margarine (butter optional)
3 qts.	hot water
1 pkg.	Angus mix, 3/4 oz.
1 tsp.	salt
1 tsp.	black pepper
1/2 cup	Worcestershire sauce
1 Tbl.	onion powder
1 tsp.	granulated garlic
	croutons
	Swiss cheese, grated

Procedure

Saute onions in margarine until transparent and then remove from heat. Mix all other ingredients together and bring to a hard boil. Add onions and cook for 1 minute and remove from heat. Serve in bowls topped with croutons and Swiss cheese.

TOMATO & BACON DRESSING

1/2 cup	salad oil
1/2 cup	olive oil
1/2 cup	white vinegar
1/2 cup	red wine vinegar
1/2 cup	Coco-cola
1 tsp.	thyme
1 tsp.	onion powder
1 tsp.	sugar
1/2 tsp.	garlic, minced
1 cup	real bacon bits
2 med.	tomatoes, diced

Procedure

Mix all together and refrigerate tightly covered until needed. Stir or shake well before using.

CHICKEN DIJON SALAD

DRESSING

Ingredients

2 cups	olive oil
1 cup	white vinegar
1 cup	salad dressing
3 Tbls.	garlic, minced
1 cup	onion, minced
4 Tbls.	parsley
5 Tbls.	Dijon mustard

Procedure

Blend everything together thoroughly with a wire whip. Chill for 30 minutes. Makes 1 quart.

For less, cut recipe in half.

Salad recipe follows.

CHICKEN DIJON SALAD

First, marinate 2 chicken breasts in 1 cup of dressing for 1 hour. After marinating, roast chicken in oven at 350 degrees for 20-30 minutes and discard marinade. Remove from oven and cool in refrigerator.

Salad Ingredients: Use as much of any, or better yet, all of the following ingredients in the amount you need. This salad is excellent as a main course luncheon salad or for dinner. Simply add additional chicken and salad ingredients and you can feed a pair or a crowd.

Ingredients

romaine, iceberg, and spinach
tomato wedges
artichoke hearts
red onion
cucumber
mushrooms
green peppers

Procedure

After salad plate is prepared, take chicken breasts and slice at an angle. Top your salad with chicken and a sliced hard boiled egg. Cover with dressing.

CREAMY CRAB DRESSING

Ingredients

2 cups	sour cream
1 cup	mayonnaise
1 1/2 cups	half and half
1 Tbl.	onion powder
5 Tbls.	lobster base
12 ozs.	crab meat

Procedure

Mix all except crab meat together until smooth. Then, add the crab meat and mix well.

Chill for at least 1 hour.

Serve over your favorite salad.

BBQ SAUCE

Ingredients

2/3 cup	soy sauce
3/4 cup	mustard
2/3 cup	Worcestershire sauce
1/3 cup	salad oil
1 1/4 cup	sweet relish
2/3 tsp.	ginger
1 Tbl.	liquid smoke
2/3 tsp.	granulated garlic
2/3 Tbl.	salt
6 shakes	Tabasco
3/4 cup	crushed pineapple
2/4 cup	chili sauce
2/4 cups	ketchup

Procedure

Mix all together and use as any other fine B B Q sauce.

WHITE SAUCE

Makes 2 cups

Ingredients

1/4 cup	butter
1/4 cup	flour
2 cups	milk
1 tsp.	lemon juice
1 tsp.	salt
1/4 tsp.	white pepper

Procedure

Melt butter over low heat. Add flour, stirring constantly 3 to 4 minutes or until well blended. Stir in milk a few tablespoons at a time, blending well after each addition. Add seasonings and simmer 2 to 3 minutes or until sauce thickens. Continue to cook 2 to 3 minutes more while blending with a wire whisk, if necessary, to get desired smoothness.

TARTAR SAUCE

Makes 1 cup

Ingredients

1 cup	mayonnaise
1 1/2 Tbls.	shallots, finely minced
2 Tbls.	dill *or* sweet pickles, finely chopped
1 Tbl.	fresh parsley, finely chopped
1 tsp.	lemon juice
1/8 tsp.	cayenne pepper
	black pepper, freshly ground to taste

Procedure

Combine all ingredients in a small mixing bowl, mix well, cover and chill for at least 1 hour.

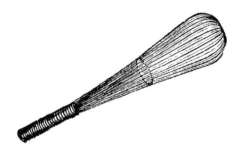

NEW ORLEANS HOUSE

CAJUN SPICE

This spice is available at the restaurants

This spice can be used for cooking or as a blackened spice for fish, chicken or beef.

Ingredients

6 Tbls.	paprika (Spanish)
4 Tbls.	salt
2 Tbls.	cayenne pepper
2 Tbls.	onion powder
1 Tbl.	oregano
1 Tbl.	basil
1 Tbl.	thyme

Procedure

Mix all together thoroughly.

Depending on your personal tolerance for hot food, there are 2 ways to use this spice for blackening. After dipping food in butter, and skillet is very hot and ready to use:

1. Sprinkle spice on food = mild
2. Roll food directly in the spice = hot

Then lay food into skillet carefully. Cook for required time for food and carefully turn over.

CAUTION: Cooking blackened food creates smoke.

ROUX - THICKENING FOR

CREAM SAUCES

Ingredients and procedure

1 1/2 lbs.   butter
               flour

Completely melt butter in a saute pan. Add flour 1/4 cup at a time until you get the consistency of mayonnaise.

WHITE SAUCE

Makes 2 quarts

Add together in a 5 quart saucepan on medium heat.

1/2 gal.	milk
1/2 Tbl.	garlic powder
1/2 Tbl.	onion powder
1 tsp.	salt
1/4 tsp.	white pepper
1/4 cup	Parmesan cheese, grated

Procedure

Once milk mixture is steaming hot, stir in roux 1/3 cup at a time. Wait 1 minute then add another 1/3 cup of roux. Continue this procedure until you get the consistency of pudding. Remove from heat. To make less, cut the recipe in half.

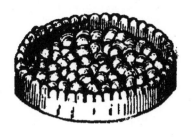

DESSERT RECIPES

FROM THE

NEW ORLEANS HOUSE

RESTAURANTS

CHOCOLATE COVERED

CHERRY PIE

Ingredients

1	pie crust, baked
1 qt.	heavy cream
1 cup	sugar
2 cups	real chocolate chips
2 Tbls.	cocoa powder
2 Tbls.	imitation vanilla
1 cup	corn starch
1 cup	whole milk
1 cup	maraschino cherries

Procedure

Layer the cooked pie crust with the cherries.

Heat cream in a medium size pot. Add sugar and mix. When cream is steaming hot, add vanilla, cocoa, and chocolate chips.

In a separate bowl, mix corn starch and milk together thoroughly.

When cream is steaming hot, add half the corn starch mixture, (stirring constantly). Keep adding corn starch until you get a pudding look. Remove from heat. Pour the pudding mixture over the cherries.

Refrigerate for 1 1/2 hours before serving.

AMBROSIA

Ingredients

Frosting:

1 qt.	whipping cream
2 Tbls.	cocoa powder
1/2 cup	granulated sugar
3 ozs.	Grand Marnier

Procedure

Whip first 3 ingredients until stiff and forms peaks.
Slowly fold in the 3 ozs. of Grand Marnier.

Cake:

Ingredients

1 box	brownie mix, grocery bought
2 cups	cocoa bits, Toll house
	chopped walnuts to taste
1 jar	Hershey's fudge

Procedure

Follow directions on package of brownie mix and
prepare. Bake in a 13 x 9" pan.

After brownies are cooled, cut the one piece in half. Thinly spread top with Hershey's fudge, sprinkle with one half of the cocoa bits. Next, lay the second half of the brownie on top of the first. Then, spread another thin layer of fudge on top of second half and sprinkle with remaining cocoa bits. Next, spread frosting over sides and top of fudge covered brownie. Last, sprinkle walnuts on top.

Refrigerate. Set out about 15 minutes before serving.

CREME BRULEE

Ingredients

6	eggs
1/2 cup	sugar
1 Tbl.	vanilla
1/2 qt.	milk

Procedure

Mix together thoroughly and divide into 6 small custard cups.

Place cups in a pan filled with water to cover 3/4 of the outside of the cups. Cover with foil and bake at 350 degrees for 45 minutes.

Remove from the water bath and top with a thin layer of brown sugar, and then place the cups under broiler, just until sugar melts. Serve hot.

NEW ORLEANS PIE

Ingredients

2	eggs
1 cup	sugar
1/4 cup	butter
1 tsp.	vanilla
1/2 cup	flour
3/4 cup	semi-sweet chocolate chips
1 cup	walnuts, chopped
1/2 cup	walnuts, chopped for topping
3/4 cup	semi-sweet chocolate chips for topping

Procedure

Beat eggs well and slowly add sugar, butter, vanilla and flour. Remove from beater. Stir in chocolate chips and walnuts. Grease an 8 inch pie pan and pour in batter. Preheat oven to 350 and bake for 30 minutes or until inserted knife comes out clean. Let pie cool for 30 minutes. Melt chips for topping. Spread a thin layer of fudge topping on pie.

Sprinkle lightly with walnuts for topping.

MISSISSIPPI MUD PIE

Ingredients

2 cups	sugar
1 cup	margarine
4	eggs
2 Tbls.	cocoa
1 tsp.	vanilla
1/4 tsp.	coconut flavoring
1 1/2 cups	flaked coconut
1 1/2 cups	flour
1 tsp.	baking powder
1 1/2 cups	pecans
1 jar	marshmallow creme, 7 oz.

Procedure

Cream sugar, butter cocoa and eggs. Beat well. Add vanilla, coconut flavoring, flour and baking powder. Mix well. Add coconut and nuts. Spread mixture in greased 9x13" baking dish. Bake at 350 degrees for 30 minutes. While pie is still hot, spread top with the marshmallow creme. Cool pie, then cover with frosting

Recipe for frosting see next page

Frosting:

Ingredients

1/3 cup	evaporated milk
1 tsp.	vanilla
3 Tbls.	cocoa
3/4 stick	margarine
1/2 box	powdered sugar, 8 ozs.

Procedure

Sift powdered sugar and cocoa together. Cream the margarine into the sugar mix. Add the vanilla and slowly add the milk, mixing all the time. Spread over top of pie using a flat spatula. Tap top of frosting lightly with the back of a spoon to raise frosting into small peaks.

APPLE ORLEANS

Ingredients

Peel core and slice 1 lb. of apples and put in a bowl.
In a separate bowl combine:

6 Tbls.	cornstarch
5 Tbls.	melted butter, (blend with a whisk)
1/2 cup	honey, (blend with a whisk)
1 Tbl.	lemon juice
1/2 Tbl.	cinnamon
1/2 tsp.	ground cloves
1/8 tsp.	salt

Procedure

Blend all ingredients with whisk until creamy. Pour
over apples stirring until they are all coated. Place in
a 9x12" baking dish.

Cover with Strudel Topping made as follows:

Ingredients

2 cups	flour
1 cup	brown sugar
1/2 lb.	cold butter, cubed in small pieces
1 tsp.	ginger
1 cup	walnuts

Procedure

Cut first four ingredients with a pastry blender until
evenly crumbly. Add walnuts mixing in by hand.
Spread topping evenly over the apples.
Bake at 300 degrees for 35 to 40 minutes.

BANANA SPLIT DESSERT

Ingredients

1/3 lb.	graham crackers
2 cups	powdered sugar
4	bananas
1 lg. pkg.	cool whip
	maraschino cherries
3 sticks	margarine
2	eggs
8 ozs.	crushed pineapple (drained)
	nuts, chopped
	chocolate syrup to drizzle

Procedure

Make Graham Cracker Crust with crumbs and 1 stick of margarine, (melted). Press into 2 quart baking dish. Chill.

Beat together powdered sugar, 2 sticks margarine and eggs with electric mixer for at least 15 minutes. Spread mixture over graham cracker crust. Let chill for 2 hours.

Before serving, slice bananas to cover top of dessert. Then spread whipped topping over bananas. Top with Maraschino Cherries and chopped nuts. Drizzle with chocolate syrup.

EASY TO MAKE

STOCKS

STOCKS TO MAKE AT HOME

If doing your own filleting, you might at this time be interested in making fish stock with all that is left after you have extracted the parts you are interested in for your particular recipe. Bouillon and canned broth simply cannot compare to home made fish stock as you will see once you have made and used your own. This is an easy process that takes advantage of your leftovers and provides you with a delicious, fresh homemade base for all types of sauces, stews, rice dishes and soups. The making of the stock is as easy as can be, and when the stock is refrigerated the fat will solidify and rise to the top so as to be easily removed. Removing the small layer of fat and holding back on the use of salt results in a base that is virtually fat AND salt free. This is to be compared to store bought stock, some of which contains half or more of the recommended daily amounts of salt as recommended by nutritionists.

In order to accumulate enough bones to make a really good stock, save bones in a plastic storage bag in the freezer until you have enough to work with.

BASIC FISH STOCK

Makes about 2 1/2 quarts.

The fish head and bones that remain once a fish has

been filleted, from a lean, white-fleshed fish such as red snapper, halibut, flounder are known as frames. Red snapper makes a particularly tasty stock that can be used with most fish stock recipes.

Ingredients

3 1/2 lbs.	red snapper frames
1 1/2 Tbls.	olive oil
2 med.	leeks, white and pale green, thinly sliced
1	shallot, thinly sliced
1 sm.	celery rib, thinly sliced
3 sprigs	fresh thyme
2 sprigs	fresh parsley
1/2 cup	dry white wine
1	bay leaf
1 med.	tomato, chopped
	kosher salt

Procedure

Rinse the fish frames thoroughly under cold water. In a large nonreactive saucepan or small stockpot, warm the olive oil over moderate heat. Add the leeks, shallots, celery, thyme, parsley and fish frames. Bend the frames if necessary to fit them into the pot. Cook all, stirring occasionally, until the frames turn white and the vegetables are fragrant, about 4 minutes.

Add the wine and cook for 1 minute. Add 2 1/2

quarts of water, the bay leaf, the tomato and salt to taste. Increase the heat to moderately high, bringing to a gentle simmer. Skim and reduce the heat to low. Simmer the stock for 20 minutes, skimming often.

Slowly pour the stock through a fine strainer into a large heat proof bowl, leaving any particles at the bottom of the pan. Season with salt if needed and let cool before refrigerating. After completely cooled, remove small layer of fat that has risen to the top of the storage container.

CHICKEN STOCK

Makes 2 qts.

This is probably the easiest and most popular of all stocks and can be used in meat, seafood or chicken dishes with great results.

Ingredients

6 lbs.	chicken bones
3 ribs	celery, cut into 2" pieces
2 med.	carrots, cut into 2" pieces
2 med.	onions, unpeeled and quartered

Procedure

Combine all of the ingredients with 3 quarts of cold

water in a large saucepan or small stockpot and bring to a boil over high heat. Reduce heat to moderate and simmer for 20 minutes, skimming frequently. Reduce the heat to low and cover partially, leaving only a small opening between the lid and the pan. Simmer until the stock is flavorful, about 2 1/2 hours.

Slowly pour the stock through a fine strainer into a large heat proof bowl, leaving any particles at the bottom of the pan. Press on the solids to extract as much liquid as possible. Return the stock to the cleaned pan and boil until reduced to 2 quarts. Let cool completely before refrigerating. When completely cool remove layer of fat from the top for a more fat free stock.

VEGETABLE STOCK

Makes 2 quarts.

Ingredients

2 ribs	celery, coarsely chopped
3	carrots, coarsely chopped
1 med.	leek, coarsely chopped
1 lg.	onion, quartered
1 lg. bunch	spinach, (about 1 lb.)
1 lg. sprig	fresh thyme

1 bunch	fresh flat-leaf parsley
2	unpeeled garlic cloves, halved lengthwise
12	whole black peppercorns

Procedure

Combine all of the ingredients and 4 quarts of water in a large saucepan or small stockpot and bring to a boil over high heat. Cover partially, reduce the heat to moderately low and simmer until the broth is flavorful and reduced to 2 quarts, about 1 1/2 hours.

Slowly pour the stock through a fine strainer into a large heat proof bowl, leaving behind any particles at the bottom of the pan; press lightly to extract the liquid. Let cool completely before refrigerating.

BEEF STOCK

Remove the morrow from large bones thus cutting down on the amount of skimming you will have to do.

Ingredients

2 Tbls.	vegetable oil
4 lbs.	beef shanks, stripped of meat, cut crosswise
1 med.	onion, chopped
1 lg.	carrot, thickly chopped
1 med.	celery rib, thickly sliced
1 head	garlic, halved crosswise

2 tsp.	kosher salt
6 stems	fresh parsley
3 sprigs	fresh thyme
3	allspice berries
1	bay leaf
1 Tbl.	dried porcini mushrooms

Procedure

Preheat oven to 450 degrees. Warm the oil in a large flameproof roasting pan set over 2 burners on high heat. When oil is hot, add the beef shank bones and the meat. Cook, stirring until the meat starts to brown, about 3 minutes. Set the pan on the bottom shelf of the oven and roast for about 25 minutes, or until the meat and the bones are deeply browned. Add the onion, carrot, celery and garlic and stir well. Return the pan to the bottom shelf and roast for about 20 minutes, or until the vegetables are deeply browned around the edges.

Scrape the contents of the roasting pan into a large saucepan or small stockpot. Set the roasting pan over 2 burners on moderate high heat. When very hot, add 1 cup of water and scrape up the browned bits on the bottom of the pan. Boil the liquid for about 2 minutes and then pour it into the saucepan/stockpot.

Add 3 1/2 quarts of water, the salt, parsley, thyme, allspice, bay leaf and mushrooms. Bring to a boil over high heat and skim. Reduce heat to low and simmer the stock, skimming often, until deep brown and flavorful, about 1 1/2 hours. Season with a little salt, if desired. Slowly pour the stock through a fine strainer into a large heat proof bowl, leaving behind any particles at the bottom of the pan; press lightly on the solids to extract the liquid. Let cool before refrigerating. When cool, lift off the fat that will rise to the top.

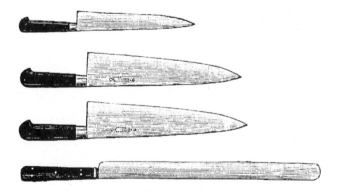

APPENDIX

OVEN TEMERATURES

BELOW 300 degrees F.   = very slow
300 degrees F.   = slow
325 degrees F.   = moderately slow
350 degrees F.   = moderate
375 degrees F.   = moderately hot
400 / 425 degrees F.   = hot
450 / 475 degrees F.   = very hot
500 degrees F.   = extremely hot

TABLE OF EQUIVALENTS

(VOLUME AND WEIGHT)

All measures are level

3 teaspoons	= 1 tablespoon
16 tablespoons	= 1 cup
2 tablespoons butter	= 1 ounce
4 tablespoons flour	= 1 ounce

1 tablespoons (Tbl.)	= 3 teaspoons (tsp.)
	= 0.5 fluid ounces (oz.)
	= 14.8 milliliters
1 cup	= 16 tablespoons
	= 0.5 pint (pt.)
	= 8 fluid ounces
2 cups	= 1 pint
	= 16 fluid ounces
	= 236.6 milliliters
4 cups	= 1 quart (qt.)
	= 32 fluid ounces
	= 0.9436 liter
1 pint	= 2 cups
	= 0.5 quart
	= 4.73 deciliters
	= 0.4732 liter
1 quart (qt.)	= 4 cups
	= 2 pints
	= 1.06 liters
1 gallon (gal.)	= 4 quarts
	= 3.79 liters

WEIGHT IN COMMON UNITS

1 ounce	= 28.35 grams
1 pound (lb.)	= 16 ounces
	= 453.59 grams
	= 0.45 kilograms
1 gram	= 0.035 ounce
1 kilogram	= 2.2 pounds

DEEP-FAT FRYING

A rule of thumb when deep-fat frying without a thermometer is to place a 1 inch cube of bread in the hot fat. The length of time it takes to turn the cube golden brown will be your guide.

345 to 355 degrees will take about 65 seconds

350 to 365 degrees will take about 60 seconds

375 to 385 degrees will take about 40 seconds

385 to 395 degrees will take about 20 seconds

APPROXIMATE CAN SIZE

Can size	Weight	Contents
6 ounce	6 ounces	3/4 cup
8 ounce	8 ounces	1 cup
Number 1	11 ounces	1 1/3 cups
12 ounce	12 ounces	1 1/2 cups
Number 303	16 ounces	2 cups
Number 2	20 ounces	2 1/2 cups
Number 2 1/2	28 ounces	3 1/2 cups

INDEX

DRESSINGS, SAUCES & SPICES

Chicken Dijon Salad Dressing	167
Creamy Crab Dressing	169
BBQ Sauce	170
New Orleans House Cajun Spice	173
Roux - Thickening for Cream Sauces	174
Tartar Sauce	172
Tomato & Bacon Dressing	166
White Sauce	171

DESSERTS

Apples Orleans	183
Ambrosia	177
Banana Split Dessert	184
Chocolate Covered Cherry Pie	176
Creme Brulee	179
Mississippi Mud Pie	181
New Orleans Pie	180

MEATS

Cajun Gumbo & Andouille Sausage	161
Chicken Dijon Salad	168
Chicken Rouxard with Roasted Garlic Butter Sauce	157
New Orleans Chicken	160

SEAFOOD

Baked Filet of Salmon with Fondue of Leeks and Roasted Garlic	105

Baked Fish	50
Baked Fish with Curried Pecan Topping	29
Baked Salmon with Mustard and Tarragon	153
Baked Scallops with Orange Sections	82
Beer Batter Fish	96
Blackened Salmon with Creamy Tomato Sour Cream Salsa Sauce	131
Boston Clam Chowder	60
Broiled Fillets with Fresh Mint	143
Broiled Salmon with Rosemary	145
Catfish with Bacon and Onions	133
Chilled Crab and Avocado Soup	86
Cornmeal-Crusted Salmon with Yogurt Sauce	129
Clams Casino	34
Crab Cakes with Chipotle Sauce	103
Crab Demos	112
Crab Meat Casserole	118
Cranberry-Glazed Salmon with Wild Rice, Herbs and Pecans	113
Creamed Smoked Salmon and Leeks	111
Curried Softshell Crabs	109
Easy New England Clam Chowder	127
Fettuccine with Sword Fish and Red Wine Sauce	107
Fish and Cheese	139
Fishsteaks with Orange	89
Fish Stew with Bay Leaves	97
Fresh Fish with Sesame Teriyaki Linguine	138
Grilled Fresh Fish with Teriyaki Glaze	87
Grilled Scallops and Pancetta with Balsamic Mignonette	85
Grilled Swordfish with Orange Salsa	77
Herb-Coated Crab Cakes	151
Italian Style Breaded Fish	33
Lobster Bisque	117
Lobster Newburg	46
Lobster Salad with Lemon Grass	119
Molded Shrimp	56
Mousse of Scallops with Saffron	137
Mussels in Wine Sauce	98

Mussels Marinara 121
New England Crab Cakes with
       Honey Dijonaise Sauce 123
New England Fish Chowder 136
New Orleans Spicy Lemon Shrimp 125
Orange Flavored Crab Cakes with
       Tomato Relish 115
Orangey Orange Roughy 81
Oven Fried Trout 100
Oysters Rockefeller 135
Paupiettes of Sole with Shrimp 71
Peppercorn Crusted Salmon
       with White Wine Sauce 57
Poached Salmon Steaks with
       Lemon-Mustard Sauce 79
Quick Bouillabaisse 43
Red Snapper with Fresh Tomato Sauce 28
Roulade of Salmon in Scallop Mousse with
       Tarragon Butter Sauce 93
Salmon Coquettes with Cheese Sauce 91
Salmon Loaf with Tomato Dill Sauce 83
Salmon Tomato Saute with Linguine 140
Salmon with Lemon Chive Cream Sauce 101
Scallop Alfredo 141
Scalloped Oysters 75
Scallops in White Wine 25
Scallop Nicoise 67
Scallop Stuffed Shrimp 73
Sea Bass with Lemon-Nut Crust 63
Seafood and Vegetable Stew
       with Spicy Rice 6
Seafood Diablo 148
Seafood Fettuccine 149
Shrimp and Crab Cannelloni 47
Shrimp Fettuccine 110
Shrimp Nicoise 132
Shrimp on a Stick 147
Shrimp Scampi 150
Simple Baked Clams 27
Smoked Fish Spread 42
Smoked Salmon Roulades 24

Smoked Salmon Salad   122
Smoked Salmon Sandwiches with
        Capers and Red Onion Relish   69
Snapper Supreme   31
Softshell Crab Casino   99
Softshell Crab Meniere   30
Softshell Crab with Toasted Pecan Butter   39
Spiced Shrimp   41
Spicy Crab and Shrimp Soup   55
Spicy Prawns   142
Stir-Fried Scallops   88
Swordfish Steaks in Green
        Peppercorn Sauce   61
Swordfish with Tomato Vinaigrette   53
Tilefish en Papillote   51
Tomato Crown Fish   38
Tuna Waldorf Salad   155
Warm Mussel and Bacon Salad with
        Anchovy Dressing   35

STOCKS

Basic Fish Stock   188
Beef Stock   192
Chicken Stock   190
Vegetable Stock   191

VEGETABLES

Bayou Green Beans   163
French Onion Soup   165
Stuffed Celery   164

NOTES

NOTES

NOTES

NOTES